Annual Update

2015

G000167867

UK Government & Politics

Neil McNaughton

Eric Magee

PHILIP ALLAN FOR

HODDER EDUCATION

AN HACHETTE UK COMPANY

Philip Allan, an imprint of Hodder Education, an Hachette UK company,
Market Place, Deddington, Oxfordshire OX15 0SE

Orders
Bookpoint Ltd, 130 Milton Park, Abingdon, Oxfordshire OX14 4SB
tel: 01235 827827
fax: 01235 400401
e-mail: education@bookpoint.co.uk

Lines are open 9.00 a.m.–5.00 p.m., Monday to Saturday, with a 24-hour
message answering service.

You can also order through the Hodder Education website:
www.hoddereducation.co.uk

© Neil McNaughton and Eric Magee 2015

ISBN 978-1-4718-3340-3

First printed 2015

Impression number 5 4 3 2 1

Year 2018 2017 2016 2015

All rights reserved; no part of this publication may be reproduced, stored in a
retrieval system, or transmitted, in any other form or by any means, electronic,
mechanical, photocopying, recording or otherwise without either the prior
written permission of Hodder Education or a licence permitting restricted
copying in the United Kingdom issued by the Copyright Licensing Agency Ltd,
Saffron House, 6–10 Kirby Street, London EC1N 8TS.

Typeset by Integra Software Services Pvt. Ltd., Pondicherry, India

Printed by CPI Group (UK) Ltd, Croydon, CR0 4YY

Hachette UK's policy is to use papers that are natural, renewable and recyclable
products and made from wood grown in sustainable forests. The logging
and manufacturing processes are expected to conform to the environmental
regulations of the country of origin.

Contents

Chapter 1

2014 euro-elections: an earthquake in British politics?

Exam success

The up-to-date facts, examples and arguments in this chapter will help you to produce good quality answers in your AS unit tests in the following areas of the specifications:

Edexcel	AQA	OCR
Unit 1	**Unit 1**	**Unit F851**
Elections	Electoral systems	Electoral systems and referenda

Context

The elections for UK members of the European Parliament were held on 22 May 2014. The following table shows the results. Small parties winning no seats are not included.

Table 1.1 UK European election results, May 2014

Party*	% of vote	Change since 2009	Seats awarded	Change of seats since 2000	% of seats awarded
UKIP	26.6	+10.6	24	+11	32.9
Labour	24.4	+9.2	20	+7	27.4
Conservative	23.0	−3.8	19	−6	26.0
Green	6.9	−0.9	3	+1	4.1
Scottish National Party	2.4	+0.3	2	–	2.7
Liberal Democrat	6.6	−6.7	1	−10	1.4
Sinn Fein	1.0	+0.2	1	–	1.4
Democratic Unionist	0.8	+0.2	1	–	1.4
Plaid Cymru	0.7	−0.1	1	–	1.4
Ulster Unionist	0.5	–	1	–	1.4

The electoral system used was the regional list. The parties offer lists of candidates in each of the regions of the UK. Voters vote for a party list rather than individual candidates. Seats are awarded broadly in proportion to the votes cast for each party, though there is some distortion owing to the regional nature of the election.

The striking features of these results were:

- The most significant outcome was the performance of the UK Independence Party (UKIP). The party had done well in the previous election of 2009, but this was put into the shade by what happened in 2014. Their share of the vote rose by over 10%, increasing their number of seats by 11. UKIP won nearly a third of the UK seats in the parliament. UKIP came top of the poll, the first major election won by a third party since the 1920s.
- The Liberal Democrats suffered a catastrophic result. The proportion of the vote won was halved since 2009 and they lost ten out of their 11 seats. After the election there was only one Liberal Democrat member in the European Parliament.
- Labour increased its share of the vote by over 9%, gaining an additional seven seats. Forecasts suggested they would win more and the party hoped to beat UKIP, but it fell short of these expectations.
- As expected it was a poor result for the Conservatives who lost nearly 4% of their 2009 share of the vote, along with six seats. However the forecasts suggested a worse result was likely so this was not as bad for the party as expected.
- None of the other small parties, including nationalists, made significant gains or losses.

What happened to the main parties?

The rise of UKIP

UKIP does tend to do better in European elections than in those that concern domestic politics. This is to be expected. The electorate's attention is focused on the issue of British membership of the EU. Those who consider themselves to be eurosceptics may well vote for UKIP to demonstrate their belief, but would possibly not vote in the same way at a general election when they are choosing a government.

However, by any standards this was an extraordinary performance by UKIP, and especially by its leader, Nigel Farage. It came on the back of a general increase in the party's popularity, as demonstrated by public opinion polls. UKIP has also recently been gaining seats in local government.

Labour

The performance of Labour was disappointing, given the unpopularity of the coalition and the fact that public opinion is gradually moving in favour of British membership of the EU and Labour is a pro-European party. At this stage of the electoral cycle, the main opposition party ought to have been winning elections, not coming second. In terms of the popular vote Labour only beat the Conservatives by 1.4%. This kind of lead, if replicated in a general election, would probably result in a Labour government, but with only a slender parliamentary majority. The unpopular leadership of Ed Miliband was largely blamed for the party's mediocre performance.

Conservatives

The main emotion felt by Conservatives was relief. Long before this election the party had accepted it would lose to UKIP, but their vote held up reasonably well. Governing parties tend to be punished by the electorate for their mistakes in such midterm elections, but it does not mean they will do as badly in a general election, when many of its traditional supporters will return. The key issue for the party was that they ran Labour so close. If they can improve their position by 2015 there is a possibility they could avoid defeat. However, the strong performance of UKIP will affect Conservatives more than Labour, so the news was also bad for the party. If UKIP can retain even half its vote in the general election of 2015, the Conservatives will almost certainly go down to defeat.

Liberal Democrats

It was clear, well before this election, that the Liberal Democrats would take a beating. Few, however, expected the scale of their defeat to be so dramatically large. Three factors were in play here:

- From the first year of the election the Liberal Democrats have been unpopular, largely because of the party's 'betrayal' of the electorate over university tuition fees.
- Nick Clegg was suffering personal unpopularity in opinion polls. He has been seen as a weak leader.
- The Liberal Democrats are the most pro-European of the parties. Given the low turnout at European elections, it is to be expected that the majority of those who vote are eurosceptics. Pro-Europeans are less likely to vote. Thus Liberal Democrats are bound to suffer. Nevertheless such factors cannot disguise the fact that this was near meltdown for the party.

The implications for the Liberal Democrats are serious. Anything like a repeat performance in 2015 will mean that the party will lose almost all its parliamentary seats. It also means that they will be unable to hold the balance of power and so will not be included in a new coalition.

Do European elections matter?

Yes, they matter

- They represent an important measure of opinion one year before the next general election. They can be seen as superior to opinion polls as they show how people *actually* vote, rather than their voting intentions.
- In the case of UKIP, they suggest that the party may well be electable. In other words people may view this result as a breakthrough. Some doubters may well be encouraged to vote UKIP in future, believing that their vote will not be wasted.
- They may have an effect on the morale of the parties. The Liberal Democrats may have been dealt a death blow, but UKIP activists and supporters will be

very encouraged. Labour will be disappointed and the position of Ed Miliband may be undermined.

- Specifically, the UKIP triumph may have an impact on Conservative policy. There is a precedent for this. In 1989 the Green Party won 15% of the vote in the European election of that year. This did not convert into significant gains elsewhere, but it did shock the three main parties into adopting more ecologically friendly policies to capture some of the Greens' support. The Conservatives, who have already promised a referendum on British EU membership, may adopt a rather more eurosceptic position. They may also be forced to take a harder line on immigration to take away some of UKIP's ground. It may also be the case that Labour and/or the Liberal Democrats will ultimately be forced to offer such a referendum to the electorate.

No, they do not matter

- At 34%, the turnout in this election was low. This suggests it is not an accurate reflection of wider political opinion in the UK. As we have said above, many eurosceptics use it as an opportunity to promote their view, while many pro-Europeans did not vote.
- The electorate know that they are not electing a government. Many voters will support a party they would not vote for in a general election. A significant proportion of the UKIP vote can be seen in this way. Liberal democrats also hope that their support will recover in the general election.
- UKIP may have increased its representation in the European Parliament, but they remain part of the minority in that Parliament (where left of centre groupings have a majority). It also has to be said that, though its powers have increased in recent years, the European parliament remains a marginal influence on European Union policy making.

What does it say about 2015?

Of course if these results were reproduced in the next general election, there would be a seismic shift in British politics, the like of which has never been seen before. But this will not happen. Nevertheless we can draw some conclusions:

- UKIP now probably have enough solid support to have hopes of winning some seats in the UK Parliament. This is unlikely to be decisive, but it will affect the two main parties.
- If UKIP take a significant number of votes away from Conservative candidates in marginal seats in 2015, it will result in the loss of many such seats, largely to Labour.
- On the other hand if UKIP can capture Labour votes, it will reduce Labour's chance of winning an overall majority.
- The collapse of Liberal Democrat support may change the whole political landscape. If the party loses most of its parliamentary seats, there is unlikely to be a hung parliament and therefore there will be no coalition government after 2015.
- The combination of the UKIP surge and the Liberal Democrat collapse, on balance, looks likely to favour the Labour Party.

What they said about the result

Nigel Farage

[This has been] The most extraordinary result that has been seen in British politics for 100 years...the people's army of UKIP have spoken tonight.

David Cameron

The European Parliament is important but people do see it as an opportunity to send a message, and a variety of messages to the Government.

I take a very clear message from the election. People are deeply disillusioned with the EU. They don't feel the current arrangements are working well enough for Britain and they want change. I would say that message is absolutely received and understood.

Nick Clegg

There has been a very sharp turn, not only here but across Europe, to the right and in some cases the far right and uniquely, certainly in British politics, the Liberal Democrats have decided to take on UKIP and argue for the things we believe in, a generous hearted, an open minded, an internationalist Britain. It didn't work, but it was right that we stood up for the values we believe in.

Summary

The question posed is whether the European election results represent an earthquake in British politics. The answer is almost certainly 'no'. Partly because of the first-past-the-post electoral system, that prevents smaller parties making a breakthrough in terms of seats won and partly because many voters will change their choice between 2014 and 2015, UKIP will not retain their position. Similarly, it seems unrealistic to assume that the Liberal Democrats will perform so badly again. As we have said above, the apparent Green Party 'breakthrough' in 1989 did not convert into parliamentary change.

Yet something significant has happened and we can say there has been a tremor, a tremor which will be felt by all the main parties, especially the Conservatives. The centre of gravity of British politics may shift to the right. This means a more eurosceptic position, and harder lines on immigration control and law and order issues. We may also see several UKIP MPs elected in 2015 and this may destabilise the Conservative Party. The defections of Douglas Carswell and Mark Reckless to UKIP, and their subsequent election in by-elections in Clacton and Rochester and Strood, respectively, may well be the harbinger of further shifts on the right of British politics.

One other major change may be on the horizon. Since 1997 it can be argued that Britain has been a three-party system. If the Liberal Democrats do not recover, and assuming UKIP only win a handful of parliamentary seats, Britain will once again be a two-party system.

Exam focus

To consolidate your knowledge of this chapter, answer the following questions:

1 Has the UK Independence Party made a decisive breakthrough in British politics?
2 How do elections using the regional list system tend to differ from elections using first-past-the-post?
3 Are the Liberal Democrats in terminal decline?
4 Do elections, other than general elections, matter?

Chapter 2

Scottish independence referendum: why did the 'no' campaign win?

Exam success

The up-to-date facts, examples and arguments in this chapter will help you to produce good quality answers in your AS unit tests in the following areas of the specifications:

Edexcel	AQA	OCR
Unit 1 Democracy and political participation	**Unit 1** Participation	**Unit F851** Participation and voting
Unit 2 The UK Constitution	**Unit 2** The British Constitution	**Unit F852** The constitution

Context

During the debates about whether to devolve more power to Scotland and Wales in 1997 (which did result in the devolution Acts) it was argued by opponents that devolution would open the door to demands for full independence and might lead to the break-up of the United Kingdom. The closeness of the referendum result demonstrates how valid this argument was.

On 18 September 2014 the people of Scotland voted in a referendum held to decide whether they supported full independence from the United Kingdom. The UK government and Parliament agreed that if Scotland voted yes this would be honoured and Scotland would move quickly to full independence. However the result was a comfortable 'no'.

This chapter considers some of the reason why Scotland voted no. It also examines how successful the referendum was, whether it was democratic and whether it proved the best way to resolve such an issue.

The result

Table 2.1 Scottish independence referendum results, 2014

Yes	1,617,989	44.7%
No	2,001,926	55.3%
Turnout		84.6%

The country was divided into 32 regions for the purpose of counting and the results were published by region. These help us to understand better why the result was a 'no'. Only four regions voted yes. These included Glasgow City and Dundee City. This demonstrates that the result was widespread and not confined to any particular area. This is important as it will not lead to any pockets of discontented citizens.

How were the votes distributed?

As we have said, there was no significant regional variation in the vote. However, the early conclusions suggest the following trends:

- Elderly voters were more likely to vote no.
- Young voters, including the new electorate of 16 and 17-year-olds, who were permitted to vote in the referendum, were more likely to vote yes.
- Voters with lower incomes were more likely to vote yes.
- Wealthier voters were more likely to vote no.
- The 'no' majority was lower in urban areas compared to the countryside. In particular Glasgow and Dundee had 'yes' majorities. However, Aberdeen, very much the industrial powerhouse of Scotland, voted no.

The campaign

Up to the end of August the 'no' campaign, known as 'Better Together', was well ahead in the opinion polls. In early September, however, the opinion polls began to change. The gap between the two sides narrowed. A week before the referendum one poll, run by YouGov, showed the 'yes' campaign ahead. This completely changed the landscape. The 'no' campaign, supported by all three main English parties, had to face the possibility of defeat. A number of theories were advanced for this development:

1 The large number of undecided voters began to make up their minds and most of these were opting for 'yes'.

2 English politicians are not especially popular in Scotland and the intense involvement of such people was counterproductive. This was especially true of Labour, as research suggested that large numbers of traditional Labour voters were moving to the 'yes' side.

3 The two leaders of the 'yes' campaign – Scottish first minister Alex Salmond and his deputy, Nicola Sturgeon – were considered to be more effective than their main opponent, the leader of the 'Better Together' campaign, Alistair

Darling. This was reinforced in the second televised debate on the issue. This is examined further below.

In the final days, however, opinion reversed and began to move back towards 'no'. The theories for this new trend included:

1 The intervention of Gordon Brown, former UK prime minister and a Scottish MP, was important. He campaigned with great passion, recognising that, for many people, this is a visceral (emotional) issue rather than a rational one. He tapped into people's fears about independence and traditional attachment to the United Kingdom.

2 The final undecided voters, at the last minute, opted mostly for no change, fearing the unknown consequences of independence.

3 A large number of celebrities came out against independence. David Beckham, Eddie Izzard and Bob Geldof were notable examples.

4 A number of large banks, such as the Royal Bank of Scotland and Lloyds, threatened to move their operations out of Scotland if there was a 'yes' vote, and relocate in London. Several large companies followed suit, including Standard Life Insurance and BP.

5 Some companies warned that prices in Scotland would rise after independence. Tesco and Asda, for example, claimed this.

The final opinion polls showed that the 'no' campaign was once again moving ahead and they proved to be very accurate once the real results were known.

The televised debates

There were two televised debates between the leaders of both sides, Alistair Darling for 'Better Together' and Alex Salmond for the 'no' campaign.

- **Debate 1** was held on 5 August and was hailed as a victory for Alistair Darling and the 'no' campaign. In particular, Darling challenged Alex Salmond to say what currency an independent Scotland would use and Salmond did not have a convincing answer. The whole issue of Scotland's potential place in the EU was also questioned. After this debate opinion polls suggested the 'no' campaign was about 16% ahead of the 'yes' campaign.

- **Debate 2** took place on 25 August. It was generally acknowledged that this was won by Alex Salmond. Darling continued to talk about the issue of what currency Scotland would use even though Salmond had answers, suggesting there were at least three alternatives to a currency union with the UK. Salmond successfully argued that his country had been continually let down by Westminster politics. He also successfully argued that an independent Scotland would not have made the welfare cuts that were proving so unpopular in much of the UK. Darling found himself trying to defend policies made by the coalition government even though he is a Labour ex-minister. After the debate the 'no' campaign's lead had narrowed to about 10%, polls suggested.

The main campaign issues

The table below shows the main arguments used by the two sides, together with those that emerged as the campaign unfolded.

Table 2.2 The main arguments of the 'yes' and 'no' campaigns

The main campaign arguments	
Yes	**No**
• There was a strong historical and cultural argument that Scotland had been dominated by England for centuries and this was the opportunity for freedom. • Scotland was usually governed by parties in Westminster for whom the Scots had not voted. This was especially true of Conservative administrations. • It was claimed that the majority of Scottish people are more supportive of social justice and human rights than in the rest of the UK. In particular the campaign argued that the welfare state, the NHS especially, was under threat from the UK government. • Scotland had special qualities, such as the inventiveness and creativity of its people, which would help it to prosper. • There was general disillusionment with Westminster politics and politicians who largely ignore the interests of Scotland. • It was claimed that many of Scotland's resources, including oil and energy generally, should not be shared with the rest of the UK.	• An emotional argument urged Scots not to break the union which has lasted for centuries. • It was claimed that Scotland is too small a country to survive in the modern globalised world. • The campaign argued that Scotland has long been 'subsidised' by English taxpayers and this would be lost with independence. • It was not practicable, they suggested, for Scotland to have its own currency or to use the pound. Similarly it would be many years before they could use the euro. • Many financial institutions and other companies might move operations from Scotland into England. Unemployment would rise under independence, it was argued. • Scotland could no longer rely on the military protection of the UK. • It would be a 'leap into the unknown'.

Why did the 'no' campaign win?

It will be some time before enough research can be done to answer this question. However, some early conclusions are possible. Among the reasons are these:

■ Almost certainly the 'no' vote won because it represented a coalition of two kinds of voter. Voter type 1 was the person who did not want or feared change, who was motivated by the overwhelming desire to keep the union together. Voter type 2 may have been undecided about the importance of the union but heard the promises made by main UK party leaders to devolve significant powers to Scotland if there was to be a 'no' vote. They were, in other words, persuaded that a 'no' vote was indeed a vote for change. Had there been no such assurances it seems likely that 'yes' would have won comfortably.

■ The intervention of the leaders of all three main parties in Westminster may well have been decisive. When the opinion polls suggested the outcome would be very close, about two weeks before the vote was due the three leaders came together to make promises to the Scots that the country would receive considerable extra powers (so-called 'devo-Max') if there was a 'no' vote. They suggested that Scotland would gain considerable independence over taxation and welfare spending. This would mean that Scotland would be effectively self-governing even if it did not gain independence.

- There is no doubt that many Scots feared the unknown consequences of independence. This may have been the determining factor in the decision of many of those who were undecided until the last minute.
- The currency issue seems to have been important. The Scottish nationalists were never fully convincing about whether Scotland could use sterling. This led to fears that a Scottish currency would be weak and thus damage the economy.

Was this a successful exercise in democracy?

The answer to this has to be a resounding 'yes'. There are a number of reasons for reaching this conclusion:

Turnout

The most striking feature was the size of the turnout, at 85%. In some regions turnout was above 90%, an unprecedented figure. Research suggests that the size of the turnout was a clear indication that the majority of Scots did want some kind of change, whether it be full independence or increased devolution. It was also a reflection of the passion which was generated, notably by Alex Salmond, Nicola Sturgeon, Gordon Brown and Labour's shadow development minister, Jim Murphy, who toured the whole of the country campaigning for a 'no' vote.

Young voters

For the first time all over-16s were given the vote in this referendum. The reason for this was that the outcome would have very long-term effects so it was important the young had a say. There is much evidence that the campaign did engage these voters in a way never seen before. Conventional party politics traditionally turns young voters off. This was not the case here. It is an interesting question whether there will be a positive knock-on effect among this part of the electorate in future elections.

The conduct of the campaign

Apart from some examples of minor violence (egg throwing, scuffles, etc.), the referendum campaign was conducted in a civilised way and engaged large numbers of people in peaceful debate. Campaigners were successful in persuading voters first, that this was a key question which should involve everybody and second, that it was possibly a 'once in a lifetime' decision. Above all, voters were properly engaged by political leaders. It is a common complaint among voters that, in normal elections, political leaders seem out of touch. This was not the case in Scotland.

The conduct of the outcome

As we have said, an important feature of democracy is whether change can be achieved peacefully. The referendum showed how divided Scotland was over the issue, but this division did not translate into open conflict. The exercise of democracy ultimately proved to be peaceful.

The aftermath

The immediate result was the resignation of Alex Salmond as leader of the Scottish National Party. It is not clear the extent to which he will retire from politics in general. Salmond has been, arguably, one of the most successful British politicians in recent years. He raised the SNP to a position where it was able to form a majority government in the Scottish parliament and then brought the country to the brink of independence. He has now been succeeded as party leader and first minister by his deputy, Nicola Sturgeon, who also promises to make a striking impact. For supporters of more women in frontline politics, this represents progress. Salmond's fate, however, reinforces the well-known adage of the Conservative politician of the 1960s and 70s, Enoch Powell, that 'all political careers end in failure'.

It is a test of a successful democracy that the losers in a poll accept the right of the winners to have their way. In the days following the referendum there was an absence of major violence or discontent among the 'yes' supporters. There has been suspicion about whether the UK parties will renege on their promise to devolve significantly more powers to Scotland, but the result has been accepted. Similarly the winners should respect the interests of the losers. It has been recognised that 45% of the voters opted for independence and their voices should be heard. This is reflected in a determination to ensure that meaningful additional devolution does take place. English politicians have been forced to listen to the Scots for some time to come.

Summary

The initial question for this chapter was why Scotland voted no to independence. In a sense the importance of this question has been overtaken by many other considerations. Of these perhaps two are most significant. The first is the effect it has had on the devolution debate. This is discussed in Chapter 3 of this book. Above all, Westminster politicians were panicked into publishing a timetable for devolution which proposed that much of the legislation should be passed before the next election on 7 May 2015. The second is the impact it has had on British democracy. For the first time in decades the turnout returned to the kind of figures that have not been seen since the 1950s. Whether or not this is a turning point remains to be seen. However, it may be that the young, of Scotland at least, have become more politicised.

Two further questions remain for students of UK politics. The first is whether the Scottish experience suggests that referendums should be increasingly used as a way of securing consent, or otherwise, to constitutional change. If further devolution is proposed, to Wales, Northern Ireland, English regions and even to the large cities, it may be that we are in for many more referendums. The second is whether this question has now gone away for the foreseeable future or whether there will have to be another vote before long. Certainly if UK politicians do not deliver meaningful additional devolution, this may occur sooner than we think.

Exam focus

To consolidate your knowledge of this chapter, answer the following questions:

1 Why did the Scots reject independence?
2 To what extent does the Scottish referendum suggest that referendums are a successful way to determine political issues?
3 Does the Scottish referendum suggest that over-16s should be given the vote for all elections?
4 How, and to what extent, has the Scottish referendum opened the door to significant increases in devolution?
5 In what senses was the Scottish referendum a 'triumph for democracy'?
6 Why was the outcome of the referendum more a vote for change than a vote for no change?

Chapter 3

Devolution: what now?

Exam success

The up-to-date facts, examples and arguments in this chapter will help you to produce good quality answers in your AS unit tests in the following areas of the specifications:

Edexcel	AQA	OCR
Unit 2	**Unit 2**	**Unit F852**
The constitution	Multi-level governance	The constitution

Context

Devolution in the UK dates back to 1997–98 when Scotland, Wales and Northern Ireland all had new administrations set up, and considerable power was transferred from the central UK government and Parliament in London to these new systems. It was Scotland that received most powers. Even before 1998 Scotland controlled its own legal system (including the police) and education establishment. After 1998 it was also able to control the health service, transport, local government services, agricultural support and a host of other services. It was able to vary the level of income tax, but only by small amounts, and has never exercised that power. Wales and Northern Ireland did not receive the same range of powers.

Devolution was seen as a successful constitutional development. Demands for greater devolution, especially in Wales and Scotland, were relatively muted so it was assumed that demands for greater autonomy had been successfully addressed. All this changed dramatically in 2011. In the election to the Scottish Parliament of that year, the Scottish National Party (SNP) won an overall majority and formed a government on its own, led by First Minister Alex Salmond. The party had long since demanded a referendum on full Scottish independence. A proposal was passed in the Scottish Parliament and the British (Conservative) government was forced to grant them their demand. A referendum was agreed for 18 September 2014. The nature and outcome of this campaign are described in Chapter 2 of this Update.

Before looking at the devolution issue as it stands in 2014–15, it is vital to understand the true nature of devolution.

What is the meaning of devolution?

Devolution should not be confused with federalism. The term refers to the transfer of powers, *but not sovereignty*, to regional bodies. Devolution has a number of implications which do not apply to federalism:

- The powers that are transferred are not safeguarded; they can be reclaimed by the central authority. In other words, the UK Parliament retains legal sovereignty despite devolution.
- The different regions do not necessarily receive *equal* powers. For example, in 1997–98 more powers were transferred to Scotland than to Wales and Northern Ireland. This means it is *asymmetrical*. Federalism implies the *same* powers given to each region.
- Under federal settlements it is normal that any powers not allocated by a constitution or by legislation belong to the regions. Under devolution, any disputed powers automatically belong to the central authority, the UK Parliament.
- Federal systems tend to be permanent and difficult to alter (needing constitutional amendment). Devolution, on the other hand, is a process, not an event; the distribution of powers can be altered at any time in the future.

So, devolution refers to a process whereby powers are distributed to regions, away from the centre. As things stand, Scotland, Wales and Northern Ireland enjoy devolved powers. However, devolution may, in the future in the UK, also be granted to English regions and perhaps even to large cities.

Why are there demands for greater devolution?

This is a complex question. The election of a majority SNP government in Scotland in 2011 was an important milestone. It was interpreted to mean that the people of Scotland were pleased with the devolution they already enjoyed, but wanted more and wanted the country to enjoy more autonomy from UK government. Of course support for the SNP does indicate a degree of support for full independence (i.e. Scotland becoming a separate sovereign state), but to some extent it demonstrates no more than a desire for more devolution.

Demands for more devolution in Scotland were also the result of dissatisfaction with the way in which Scotland has been treated in recent years. Among them were these:

- Scotland was consistently lagging behind the rest of the UK in terms of economic prosperity.
- London government was seen as remote and not sensitive to Scotland's needs.
- There has also been a widespread dissatisfaction (not confined to Scotland) with the *conduct* of UK politics, including a belief that London-based politicians have failed to respond to popular demands.
- To some extent there was a demand for Scotland to be able to adopt a different kind of politics to London. In general, Scotland has been more attached to a strong state welfare system, human rights and democratic styles of parliamentary government than the rest of the UK.

- Some more radical nationalists believe that Scotland has been held back by the rest of the UK, notably in terms of energy production, innovation, education and economic investment.

These reasons have been further exacerbated by the changes that have taken place in the party system. This became acute in 2010. In the general election of that year only one Conservative MP was elected in Scotland and 11 Liberal Democrats. In other words, out of a total of 59 Scottish seats, only 12 were won by the two coalition parties. This, argue nationalists, meant that Westminster government was not legitimate. Indeed, so great is Labour's domination of general elections in Scotland (the party won 41 seats – about two-thirds of the total – in 2010), that anything other than a Labour government lacks such legitimacy. Devolution provides part of the answer to this problem.

Gordon Brown's statement on 9 September 2014 about devolution, shown below, reflects this movement.

> Quite simply, Scottish voters deserve to know to the fullest extent possible about how new powers as ambitious as possible will be delivered as soon as possible within the UK. And so we are demanding a tight timetable with tough deadlines and streamlined procedures.
>
> A 'no' vote on 18 September will not be an end point, but the starting gun for action on 19 September, when straight away we will kick off a plan to deliver the enhanced devolution that we want.
>
> On 19 September we will start bringing into law the new, stronger Scottish Parliament, and to secure the change we want we will work with the other parties. The Scottish people will expect nothing less, not only because that is the right thing to do, but because we need an agreed timetable with deadlines for delivery and a roadmap to our goal.

The Barnett Formula

The so-called Barnett Formula is an additional issue in the devolution debate. It was named after Joel Barnett, Labour Treasury minister who devised it in 1978. It was designed to be implemented if devolution to Scotland, Wales and Northern Ireland was granted in 1979. In the event, that attempt at devolution failed, but the formula has been retained and has continued to be controversial.

It should be understood first how governments in Scotland, Wales and Northern Ireland are financed. Although local taxation is retained in these countries, they do not collect any *national* taxes, which account for most of their expenditure needs. Instead, Westminster government collects all national taxes and then gives an annual grant to the three countries to pay for such services as health, education, transport and policing. The Barnett Formula calculates how much each country should receive each year. It is an extremely complicated calculation and a difficult issue, but in essence it comes down to these arguments for and against:

Opponents of the Barnett Formula (which, ironically, included Joel Barnett himself) say that the formula was based on population figures which were inaccurate in 1978, have never been updated, and have not taken account of population changes. They also argue that it takes no account of how much national tax is collected in these countries. They calculate that less tax per head is collected in Scotland, Wales and Northern Ireland than in England, yet there is greater expenditure per head in the smaller countries. This means that they receive a very large subsidy.

Supporters of the Barnett Formula argue that the smaller countries have special factors that mean they require this subsidy. For example Northern Ireland has its own special security issues, and Wales has many isolated communities that take up disproportionate amounts of expenditure. In Scotland there are greater demands on healthcare owing to endemic problems not found elsewhere and on transport, as the population of much of Scotland is so scattered. There is also an argument that Britain is a single nation and that it is desirable that the wealthier parts should subsidise the poorer.

Greater devolution will almost certainly end the Barnett Formula because the smaller countries would collect and control much more of their own tax revenues. This may well mean that the people of these countries will lose some of their 'English subsidy', placing a greater strain on their taxpayers. In other words it may result in higher taxes in the smaller countries.

Nevertheless, this remains a very complex issue and supporters of greater devolution suggest that, in the longer run, such inequalities will be ironed out. In particular, Scottish nationalists insist that, given more self-government, services will be more effectively and efficiently used so their expenditure burden will be reduced.

Prospects for further Scottish devolution

This will become a key issue in British politics in 2015 and probably beyond. It is essential that students of UK politics should follow the issue through to its conclusion. Whatever happens, the outcome of the issue will mean that the political face of the United Kingdom will be dramatically changed.

Near the end of 2014 the positions of the three main English parties plus UKIP and the Scottish National Party were as follows:

Conservative proposals

Surprisingly, perhaps, the Conservative proposals for future devolution are quite radical. The main features of their proposals are:

- Scotland would control its own rates of income tax and be able to spend the proceeds of income tax as it wishes, provided this would not offend UK laws.
- Probably Scotland should also have a share (unspecified as yet) of VAT raised in Scotland. The *rate* of VAT would continue to be set centrally and be the same throughout the UK.

- Some cash benefits available under the welfare state might be varied in Scotland. This would not include pensions, but could include other benefits, possibly, for example, housing benefits.
- A committee of all the Parliaments and assemblies of the UK to be set up. This would consider any further developments in devolution and establish relations between the various administrations.

Labour proposals

The Labour Party proposals are the least radical of the three main Westminster parties. Labour very much argues in favour of equality of services throughout the United Kingdom and so wishes to see more control from the centre than the others. However, the party does propose some additional devolution:

- The Scottish Parliament should be allowed to vary the basic rate of income tax by up to 15%. It would have control of any additional revenue. This would mean that Scotland would control about 40% of its own revenues and 60% would be controlled at Westminster.
- Some welfare benefits might be carried in Scotland. The main examples would be housing benefit and attendance allowances (benefits to families who need help with people with special physical needs).
- Increased power over strategic railway policy.
- More autonomy for Scottish local government. In particular Scottish local authorities would have power over the revenue for work programmes and have greater flexibility over planning.

Liberal Democrat proposals

It is no surprise to learn that the Liberal Democrats have perhaps the most radical proposals for devolution. These date back to 2012:

- Income tax would fall completely within the control of the Scottish Parliament and government. The Liberal Democrats call this **fiscal federalism.**
- Some other taxes, such as inheritance and capital gains tax would be devolved to Scotland.
- All local government in Scotland would be completely autonomous.
- The Scottish government would have wide borrowing powers and so be able to invest in infrastructure projects, in particular to boost employment.
- Nevertheless, unlike the Conservatives, they do not propose the devolution of welfare services.
- The proposals would mean that Scotland would control about two-thirds of its own revenues, about one-third would come in a block grant from the United Kingdom and therefore not be devolved.

Scottish National Party proposals

It goes without saying that the Scottish National Party wishes to see the maximum degree of devolution possible. The party retains its support for complete independence. In the interim, it suggests the following:

- The Scottish Parliament and government should have full control over all taxation (though not over VAT rates probably).

- They would have full borrowing powers on the open market.
- All other state activities would be devolved with the exception of defence, foreign affairs and control of the currency.

These proposals are known as **Devo Max**. They will certainly not be accepted by Westminster, but demonstrate the determination of the SNP to make Scotland as independent as possible, short of full national sovereignty.

UKIP
UKIP has not committed itself on devolution itself. It does support very strongly the idea of an independent English Parliament. In theory the party should support a large amount of devolution because it believes that England has been subsidising Wales, Scotland and Northern Ireland through tax and welfare. However, it resists being seen as an 'English party'. It wins little support in the smaller countries and so is concentrating on addressing the English Question rather than devolution itself.

Regional devolution
One of the complicating issues concerning devolution in the UK is that England is so much bigger than the other countries. This implies that one part of the UK will always be wealthier and more powerful than the rest. This can be contrasted with a country like Spain, which operates a devolved system, where the regions are of similar size and wealth.

One way round this is the divide England itself into regions and devolve powers to each of them as well as the smaller countries. If England were, for example, divided into eight regions, there would be a devolved system using eleven regions in total. London will always tend to dominate, but otherwise power would be more evenly spread.

There has also been much new discussion about devolution to the large cities, or city-regions such as London (which already has some of its own independent powers), Birmingham, Manchester, Leeds–Sheffield, Merseyside, and the North-East conurbation. Labour and the Liberal Democrats are especially interested in such a development. This type of devolution would involve cities having greater powers over issues such as housing, policing, transport, arts subsidies and even employment. In order to achieve city government there would certainly have to be more autonomy over how the central government grant is spent, but would also allow cities to borrow money on the open market (which they cannot do now) in order to create more investment, especially on transport and housing infrastructure.

The prospects for such regional devolution are examined further below.

The effects on the English (West Lothian) Question
The origin of the term 'West Lothian Question' can be traced to a Conservative minister and English MP, Enoch Powell, and a Labour MP, Tam Dalyell, whose constituency in Scotland was West Lothian, hence the name. They brought the

problem to public attention. The prospects of greater devolution, especially to Scotland, have rekindled interest in the West Lothian Question, which is now often called the 'English Question'. It is a complex issue, but its essence can be contained in the following issues. Here we will look at it in terms of Scotland, where the problem is at its most acute, although it does apply to a lesser extent in Wales and Northern Ireland:

- Because many powers are devolved to Scotland, notably over law and order, health, education and transport, the UK Parliament in Westminster has no control over these services.
- When these issues are being debated and possibly legislated upon as they apply in England, in the UK Parliament, the outcome will not apply in Scotland, but there are 59 MPs in the UK Parliament who represent Scottish constituencies who are able to speak and vote on these issues.
- It is seen as grossly unfair that MPs representing Scottish constituencies should have an influence and a vote on issues that do not concern them at all.
- Though MPs representing Scottish constituencies have a say over English health, education, policing and the like, MPs representing English constituencies do not have a say in these issues in Scotland.

If *more* power is to be devolved this problem simply grows larger and concerns even more issues. This has led to calls for an English Parliament.

An English Parliament?

The question now has boiled down to whether or not there should be an English Parliament, separate from the current UK Parliament. There are essentially three models for this:

Model 1

Effectively two parliaments. One would be a UK Parliament dealing with those issues *not* devolved to the national regions such as defence, foreign affairs, financial control, relations with the EU and national security. The other would be a smaller English Parliament dealing only with those matters that concern England, such as welfare, health, education, local government services and transport. This would cause problems over elections but, above all, it would not be clear who would form a government. Would there have to be two governments – a UK government and an English government? Further, what would happen if each government were controlled by a different party?

Model 2

Here there would be just one Parliament, like the current one, but when matters relating *only* to England were under consideration all the Welsh, Northern Irish and Scottish MPs would withdraw temporarily. There would be a temporary English parliament. When matters relating to the UK were under consideration *all* the MPs would return. This is the solution which has most support, though it has the same problem as Model 1. What if the English Parliament had a majority of one party, while the larger UK Parliament had a majority of another? The

2010–15 Parliament, for example, has a coalition majority when all UK MPs sit, but would have a Conservative majority of 61 if it only contained English MPs.

Model 3

This has been suggested by Malcolm Rifkind, a former Conservative minister and Scottish MP. It is a refinement of Model 2. Here, if there were legislation or a resolution which *only* affected England, it would require a majority of support from *both* the English MPs alone *and* of the whole House of Commons, including the Scottish, Welsh and Northern Ireland MPs. This is known as the **Double Majority** solution.

Many say none of these solutions really work so we must muddle along as we currently do. The Labour Party is certainly reluctant to accept any radical change, partly because they would find it very difficult to win a majority in an English-only Parliament. Without its large number of MPs representing Scottish and Welsh constituencies it would struggle to achieve a working majority.

In the past, the flexible, uncodified UK constitution has been able to absorb and adapt to change. The English Question, however, looks insoluble. Possibly only a majority Conservative government after 2015 would have the necessary majority and political will to make a radical change. An English Parliament would definitely be to the long-term advantage of the Conservatives.

Devolution outside Scotland

Assuming Scotland is granted more devolved powers, it may well be that there will be demands for more devolution in Wales and the English regions. There is little appetite or prospects for further devolution in Northern Ireland. The Unionists there are, on the whole, opposed to greater autonomy and they remain the majority community. In Wales, however, there will be calls for more devolution. Although nationalism is not nearly as strong in Wales as it is in Scotland, there have been calls for the Welsh Assembly to have more control over its own revenues and possibly for greater borrowing powers on the open market, but the country will have to wait in turn until the Scottish question has been resolved.

Regional devolution, either to regions or to cities, is growing in popularity as an idea. The main impetus has been a growing fear that Britain is becoming too 'London-centric'. The English cities and regions, it is claimed, have been starved of investment and have lagged behind London in terms of employment, transport and general economic development. Giving them greater control over tax revenues and borrowing would help to redress this imbalance. There are, however, a number of problems that make regional devolution difficult, including these:

- It would create another layer of government which many oppose on the grounds of expense and excessive bureaucracy.
- It may result in a greater amount of inequality in services from one locality to another.
- The last attempt to introduce devolution to the northeast region, including an elected assembly, in 2004, was rejected by nearly 80% of those who voted.

- The main parties do not see there are any votes to be gained by championing regional devolution, so the policy may lack political will.

Quasi federalism?

Though the Liberal Democrats favour some form of federal system, it looks unlikely to come about in the near future. However, if there is a considerable increase in devolution, including new powers transferred to Wales, Northern Ireland and perhaps the English regions or cities, some say this will represent **quasi federalism**. This term means that it will not be federalism in the *legal* sense – the Westminster Parliament would still be sovereign, but that it would *look* so much like a federal system that it would be one in all but name. There would be great decentralisation of power and it is difficult to foresee circumstances where the power would ever return to the centre.

Summary

The table below shows the likely timetable for change. However, it may well be extremely difficult for Westminster politicians to keep to the schedule. Many issues have to be resolved and, in Autumn 2014, there was still no consensus.

Table 3.1 Scottish devolution timeline

6 September 2014	A public opinion poll by YouGov suggested that the 'yes' to Scottish independence campaign was 2% ahead of the 'no' campaign. Panic set in among the three main UK parties.
9 September 2014	Supported by the three main UK parties, Gordon Brown, former prime minister, announced a new timetable for devolution to Scotland in order to help the 'no' campaign.
18 September 2014	The Scottish referendum on independence took place. It was a 'no' vote by 55% to 45%.
19 September 2014	The Smith Commission is set up to consider various proposals for further devolution to Scotland.
October 2014	The UK government issued a White Paper setting out the options for more Scottish devolution.
November 2014	The chosen option for further devolution is announced following the recommendations of the Smith Commission.
January 2015*	A draft bill for a new Scotland Act is published and presented to Parliament.
April 2015	Legislation has already been passed giving the Scottish government control over stamp duty (tax on the purchase of properties) plus some other land taxes. They will control the level of these taxes and will be free to spend the proceeds however they wish. This is eventually expected to amount to £2.2 billion. Scotland will also gain the power to borrow money on the open market to finance greater investment. These measures will come into effect after this date.

May 2015	UK general election. By this time the Scotland Act should have been passed although this milestone is doubtful.
April 2016	It has already been legislated that Scotland will have control of 10% of income tax raised there after this date.

*At the time of writing these are provisional milestones

If a settlement is not achieved fairly quickly there may be further trouble in Scotland. Many Scots were persuaded to vote no on the promise of further devolution. If their hopes are dashed, there may be a backlash. This would be seen immediately in the 2015 general election where many Labour MPs would lose their seats and the SNP would make gains. If this happens, as the new SNP leader, Nicola Sturgeon, has suggested, it may well be that there will be a second independence referendum in the next ten years.

If, on the other hand, further devolution is achieved reasonable rapidly, it will mark the greatest change in the structure of British government for over a century.

Exam focus

To consolidate your knowledge of this chapter, answer the following questions:

1 Why has devolution become a major issue in 2014–15?
2 Distinguish between devolution and federalism.
3 What is the Barnett Formula and why is it important?
4 What is the West Lothian Question and why is it difficult to solve?
5 What are the prospects for devolution outside Scotland?
6 What are the main differences in party proposals for future Scottish devolution?
7 Is Britain becoming a 'quasi federation'?

Chapter 4

2010–15 fixed-term parliament: has it worked?

Exam success

The up-to-date facts, examples and arguments in this chapter will help you to produce good quality answers in your AS unit tests in the following areas of the specifications:

Edexcel	AQA	OCR
Unit 2	**Unit 2**	**Unit F852**
Parliament	Parliament	The Legislature
The UK Constitution	The British Constitution	Parliamentary reform

Context

The position before 2010

Before the 2011 **Fixed-term Parliaments Act,** the way in which parliaments would come to an end and a new general election called was governed by an unwritten convention of the UK constitution. It was in the control of the prime minister, who enjoyed the **prerogative power** to dissolve parliament and order a new election.

This power was exercised on behalf of the monarch, but was not established in law, so it was only a convention. It was also a convention that a government should resign and a general election be held if that government lost a vote of no confidence in the House of Commons.

The only restriction on this was in the 1911 Parliament Act which established that a parliament could not last for more than five years (it had been seven before the Act), i.e. the prime minister could not delay dissolving parliament for more than five years. Up to 2010 most parliaments lasted between four and five years, with rare exceptions (e.g. the short parliaments of 1964–66 and February–October 1974).

The length of post-war governments (i.e. the gaps between elections) is shown in Table 4.1. It can be seen that most parliaments did not last the full five years and many scarcely reached four years.

When the coalition government was formed in 2010 following the general election of that year it was quickly determined that there was a need to establish how parliament could survive in such unusual circumstances and, if the coalition failed, how it would be dissolved.

Table 4.1 Length of parliaments since the Second World War

Year and month of dissolution	Length of parliament (years)
February 1950	4.7
October 1951	1.8
May 1955	3.7
October 1959	4.4
October 1964	5.0
March 1966	1.6
June 1970	4.3
February 1974	3.8
October 1974	0.7
May 1979	4.6
June 1983	4.1
June 1987	4.0
April 1992	4.9
May 1997	5.0
June 2001	4.1
May 2005	3.1
May 2010	5.0

Why was a fixed-term parliament introduced?

- It was a policy long since adopted by the Liberal Democrats. Its introduction was part of the deal struck between the two parties, known as the 'coalition agreement'. Liberal Democrats support fixed terms because it takes away some of the prime minister's arbitrary power. They believe it places an advantage in the hands of the government and weakens parliament.
- It was expected that coalition government might be fragile and that this would be a dangerous situation, creating uncertainty, not just in politics, but also in the economy and Britain's standing in the world. It was hoped that a fixed-term parliament would, therefore, provide some stability to the coalition.
- Liberal Democrats feared that the prime minister might use his power to dissolve parliament and call a general election as a threat, in order to dominate his junior partner. In other words, if the Liberal Democrats would not co-operate he could simply threaten a parliamentary dissolution. A fixed-term parliament would remove this power.
- It used to be the case that if a government lost its majority in the Commons its life would be threatened. Under coalition there was a strong likelihood that the partners would split from time to time. The fixed-term parliament allowed such splits to happen (which they have on a few occasions, notably over the reform of the House of Lords), without threatening the survival of the government.

■ It was felt that if the date of the next general election is known well in advance it makes the planning and administration of elections easier, especially in relation to postal ballots which are cast in advance.

The government at the time of the legislation stated clearly why it was supporting the measure:

> The introduction of fixed-term parliaments was intended to improve certainty and stability in Government, and to increase the fairness of the electoral process by removing the Prime Minister's ability to determine the date of poll.
>
> Source: government evidence to Parliament, 2010

However, in evidence to the Hansard Society, the BBC correspondent, Mark Darcy, was sceptical about the motives behind the measure:

> The move to fixed-term parliaments was more a 'political expedient' designed to protect the Liberal Democrats from being ditched by the Tories calling a snap election once their poll rating improves rather than what he called 'a desire for a perfect constitution'.
>
> Source: Hansard Society

What does the 2011 Fixed-term Parliaments Act say?

A key feature of the Act is that it is a short-term measure. Because of the sovereignty of parliament, each parliament cannot bind its successors. This means that the Act could be repealed at any time. It will only remain in force as long as Parliament wishes it. However, it now seems inconceivable that it will be repealed in the foreseeable future, so fixed-term parliaments are probably here to stay.

The terms are as follows:

1　There will be a general election on the first Thursday in May, five years after the previous general election. This means that the 2015 election will be held on 7 May. Parliament will be dissolved up to 25 days before polling day (the prime minister shall decide the length of that period).

2　Under exceptional circumstances, and with the approval of both houses of parliament, the date of the general election can be delayed by up to two months.

3　There are two circumstances where a general election may be held earlier than five years:
　　a　If the government loses a vote of no confidence in the House of Commons and this no confidence is confirmed within two weeks by another vote of the House.
　　b　If at least two-thirds of the House of Commons votes to hold an early general election.

N.B. In terms of the UK Constitution, this Act is an example of how a previously **unwritten** part of the constitution (the convention that the prime minister chooses the date of general elections) has been replaced by a **codified statute**.

What were the arguments against fixed-term parliaments?

Support for fixed-term parliaments was not universal. There are three main reservations:

1 The main argument is that it enables governments to plan more effectively for the election, adjusting their legislative programme and their economic policy to meet the requirements of the election. It may be, for example, that a government will reserve tax cuts until just before an election for maximum effect. If government is not sure of the election date, this is more difficult.

2 It could also be argued that it has become too difficult to remove an unpopular government. This is examined below in relation to the coalition government. The 2011 Act requires that there must be two votes in the Commons to demonstrate no confidence in government or a two-thirds majority for a dissolution. If the UK returns to single party government after 2015 this may be a serious problem as such a majority will be difficult to achieve. The relatively complicated arrangements for a dissolution in mid term mean that there is a possibility of confusion, delay and problems in ending a government that can no longer govern effectively. A two-thirds majority of the House of Commons may prove difficult to achieve and a government with a comfortable majority is unlikely to concede a vote of no confidence. Arguably such a circumstance occurred in the 1992–97 parliament when John Major was prime minister. Not only had the government lost its slender majority as a result of by-election defeats, resignations and defections, but the Conservative government was also in disarray over its policy towards Europe. Nevertheless a determined John Major struggled on for the full five years. Critics said this weak government was unable to deal effectively with an economic recession and, as a result, the party was hammered in the 1997 election. With a fixed-term parliament this kind of situation might become more common.

3 The certainty of the poll date may mean that the parties engage in a very lengthy election campaign.

One other issue should be mentioned. Whatever the arguments for or against fixed terms, many argued that five years was too long between elections. In most fixed-term systems (and virtually all modern democracies operate with fixed terms between elections) the period is four years (France is a notable exception where a presidential term is five years). This suggests a fear that some governments carry on too long and thus place the principle of proper accountability in jeopardy.

How has the fixed term worked under the coalition?

If we are to decide how well the fixed term has worked, we must first ask what the legislation was designed to do. Above all, it was designed to create stability in uncertain circumstances. It must also be remembered that the coalition was forged in the middle of an economic crisis. It seemed therefore essential that there should be a period of stable government, not least because the international

financial markets prefer political stability. It was also designed to protect the weaker coalition partner against the power of the prime minister to threaten coalition if they did not co-operate.

How well has it achieved these aims? We can examine the evidence thus:

- The key fact is that the coalition survived. Given the delicate state of the UK economy after 2008, many saw this as vital. If an economy is to recover, confidence is vital as well as a sense of continuity. Such confidence helps with investment, with the value of the country's currency and with the export effort. Had there been too much political instability it might well have stifled the recovery.
- Although the Liberal Democrats have been heavily criticised for their weakness on some issues, notably over university tuition fees, it is certainly true that the weaker coalition partner has been protected by the fixed term. Whenever there was a major disagreement within the coalition, there was some confidence that the split would not precipitate an election. This made it possible for internal conflict to take place without threatening the life of the government.
- There have been occasions when the prime minister could have called a 'snap' election at short notice in order to gain an advantage for his party. When, for example, the Conservative Party caught up with Labour in the opinion polls during 2012–13, he might have been tempted to go for an early election. He might also have taken advantage of the Liberal Democrat unpopularity at any time after 2011. An early election might have been to the benefit of the Conservative Party but not necessarily the country.

Summary

The effects of the fixed-term parliament cannot yet be fully assessed. We may have to wait until there have been three or more parliaments to do that. The former cabinet secretary, Gus O'Donnell, expressed this in his evidence to a Hansard Society enquiry in 2013:

> If you are trying to assess how fixed-term Parliaments work, it would be a bit like asking a six-months pregnant woman, 'How did the childbirth process go?' We have not had one single fixed-term Parliament yet, so we need that caveat.

Nevertheless a preliminary assessment can be made. Some conclusions can be attempted:

- With coalition government it may be essential to have fixed terms to protect the weaker partner.
- Fixed-term parliaments do weaken the prime minister. He can no longer threaten his own dissidents with a snap election to bring them into line. This has caused a problem for David Cameron with his eurosceptic wing.
- A government cannot manipulate circumstances in order to call an early election.
- The government has to accept whatever circumstances it faces every five years. Cameron may have preferred an early election before UKIP could gain so much ground. He will now have to struggle against them in 2015 when they are likely to be strong.

Exam focus

To consolidate your knowledge of this chapter, answer the following questions:

1 Why were fixed-term parliaments introduced after 2010?
2 Explain the arguments against fixed-term parliaments.
3 Explain the link between fixed-term parliaments and coalition government.
4 Why do Liberal Democrats support the idea of fixed-term parliaments?

Chapter 5

Liberal Democrats: closer to Labour or the Conservatives?

Exam success

The up-to-date facts, examples and arguments in this chapter will help you to produce good quality answers in your AS unit tests in the following areas of the specifications:

Edexcel	AQA	OCR
Unit 1	**Unit 1**	**Unit F851**
Party policies and ideas	Political parties	Political parties

Context

The Liberal Democrat annual party conference which took place in October 2014 was the party's last chance to define itself before the next general election. There will be further initiatives before May 2015, but the conference was a key point in the Liberal Democrats' development. The conference came at a low point for the party. In the opinion polls it was hovering at around 7%, a position it had been holding for nearly three years. At the same time there remains much talk about the prospects of a new coalition after the general election. This may prove to be pie in the sky, of course, as a 7% rating would translate into electoral meltdown. There is a chance that the Liberal Democrats may win fewer seats than UKIP and the SNP in Scotland. In other words it may not hold the balance of power in a future hung parliament. Labour or the Conservatives may well look towards UKIP or the SNP as a coalition partner before the Liberal Democrats.

Nevertheless, this is an appropriate time for Liberal Democrats to consider whether they should be in coalition with Labour or the Conservatives, a similar dilemma to the one they faced in 2010. To help this consideration it is worth exploring current Liberal Democrat thinking and policies to see whether, after over four years of coalition government, the party is closer to Labour or the Conservatives. In that respect it is important to identify which policies the party adopted simply in the interests of keeping the coalition together and which they would not have adopted had they not been in government.

The Liberal Democrat sacrifices

We can call the coalition policies that the Liberal Democrats supported only for the sake of the coalition 'sacrifices'. The list below shows the main examples:

- The cuts in welfare benefits do not sit well with the Liberal Democrat belief in social justice. The party accepted that some cuts were necessary, including a benefits cap, but they certainly would not have supported the so-called 'bedroom tax', limiting housing benefit, had they not been in coalition.

- Liberal Democrats support higher rates of tax on high earners. The current top rate of 45% is not as high as the party would prefer, their preference being 50%, possibly kicking in at £100,000 per annum rather than £150,000.

- The most notorious policy position was the Liberal Democrat's support for the rise in university tuition fees at the beginning of the coalition. This 'broken promise', not to raise tuition fees, is the main cause of the party's poor poll rating. The party accepts that students do have to contribute to their own higher education, but support a much higher subsidy from the government and therefore lower tuition fees. Some in the party would even abolish tuition fees altogether.

- The Liberal Democrat coalition ministers had to accept the way in which the huge budget deficit was to be cut. This emphasised government expenditure cuts more than tax rises. Had they not been in coalition, they would undoubtedly have preferred to increase taxation, especially on the well-off and on large, highly profitable companies. Like Labour the party was anxious to promote economic growth, through investment, in order to raise more government revenue.

Party ideologies

In examining the prospects for future coalitions involving the Liberal Democrats it is necessary to try to look beyond short term-policy positions. Instead we should examine the basic ideologies of the parties. In this way we can consider the more long-term prospects.

The tables below indicate the degree to which the Liberal Democrats' ideology is close to that of the other two parties. Table 5.3 then summarises the position, indicating whether there is a wide enough political consensus for *any* coalition to work, even one between Labour and the Conservatives.

Table 5.1 Liberal Democrat and Labour ideologies compared

Common ideas	Differences
Equal legal and political rights.	Liberal Democrats are more supportive of constitutional reform, including a codified constitution and federalism or quasi federalism for the UK.
Equality of opportunity and the removal of inherited privilege.	Liberal Democrats oppose most military intervention abroad except for humanitarian reasons. Labour are more interventionist.
Social justice – the elimination of excessive economic and social inequality.	Liberal Democrats emphasise decentralisation of power much more than Labour, in particular Liberal Democrats are more supportive of local government autonomy.

Common ideas	Differences
Strong support for the ideals of the welfare state, in particular the NHS.	Liberal Democrats have a stronger attachment to the 'European ideal'.
Support for progressive taxation as a means of redistributing income.	
Similar approaches to state intervention in economic management.	
Both see migration and some immigration as positive economic and social developments.	
Both stress the need for environmental protection.	

Table 5.2 Liberal Democrat and Conservative ideologies compared

Common ideas	Differences
Education as a means to creating more equality of opportunity.	Opposite views on the UK's position on European integration.
Support for equal rights for various sections of society.	Liberal Democrats are substantially more progressive on social and moral issues.
Reducing taxation wherever it is seen as a 'disincentive to work'.	Liberal Democrats are much more radical on constitutional reform, notably decentralisation of power.
Support for the welfare state *in principle*.	Liberal Democrats are much more radical on the redistribution of income from rich to poor.
	Liberal Democrats oppose much, but not all, private sector involvement in the welfare state.
	Liberal Democrats are much less favourable to international interventions than Conservatives.
	Liberal Democrats see most immigration as a positive economic and social development.
	Liberal Democrats support more state intervention than Conservatives in economic management.
	Liberal Democrats prefer an emphasis on restorative justice, while Conservatives stress a harder line on law and order.

Table 5.3 Consensus and adversarial issues between the three parties

Consensus issues	Adversarial issues
Protection of individual and group rights.	Britain and the European Union.
Environmental protection.	How far tax should redistribute income.
Some constitutional reform of the *centre* of UK government is required.	How much private sector involvement and market forces there should be in the welfare state.
The basic principles of the welfare state should be retained.	How much Britain should intervene in international affairs.
	To what extent should power in the UK be decentralised.
	How much autonomous power local government in the UK should have.
	The extent to which migration and immigration are positive or negative developments.
	The extent to which justice should be restorative or authoritarian in nature.

Tables 5.1 and 5.2 certainly indicate that the Liberal Democrats stand much closer to Labour than to the Conservatives. This is not just a case of *how many* common ideas the parties have; the tables suggest that there is greater agreement on *fundamentals*. Nevertheless, it could be argued that there is sufficient common ground, as shown in all three tables, for any coalition to be formed and to survive at least for some time.

The prospects

Leaving aside how many seats each of the three main parties win at the 2015 general election (as well as UKIP and the SNP in Scotland), there can be little doubt that a Liberal Democrat–Labour coalition is the most likely outcome if there is a hung parliament as there was in 2010. It should be remembered also that there are still some senior Liberal Democrats who started their political lives in the Labour Party. Vince Cable is the primary example of that, as is Shirley (now Baroness) Williams.

The Liberal Democrats were also wounded seriously by the experience of coalition government when they had to compromise on a number of principles, notably charging tuition fees to university students and NHS reform, allowing a greater degree of private sector involvement. This may well be a factor in any decisions they have to make in 2015.

A further complication exists over Britain's relationship with the European Union. The Conservatives hope to hold a referendum on continued membership in 2017. If this does take place the Liberal Democrats will be campaigning on a different side to the Conservatives. This would add to the stresses of such a coalition.

Summary

A Liberal Democrat–Conservative coalition is clearly problematic. Nevertheless the leadership of both parties insist that it remains a possibility after 2015. We can speculate about what such a coalition might entail. Table 5.4 below suggests the policies that might be agreed between the two parties and those that would cause conflict and tension.

Table 5.4 Prospects for a Conservative–Liberal Democrat coalition

Potential agreed issues	Potential causes of conflict
■ Taking more of the lower paid out of taxation. ■ Reforming the UK parliament to take account of further devolution. ■ Maintaining ambitious targets for carbon emissions control. ■ Eliminating the budget deficit.	■ Britain's relations with the EU. ■ Whether to replace the Human Rights Act with a British Bill of Rights. ■ Immigration controls. ■ Whether to raise more tax from the very wealthy. ■ Electoral reform. ■ Levels of overseas aid. ■ Tighter controls and limits on social security benefits. ■ The level of private sector involvement in the NHS.

We can see how difficult such a coalition would be. Coalition with Labour looks much more practical, provided the numbers of MPs for each allow an overall majority for such a combination. Certainly Labour and the Liberal Democrats could find a good range of policies on which to agree. Some of the main ones would include these:

■ The need to raise more taxes from the wealthy, though they may still disagree on methods (e.g. over a mansion tax or a wealth tax)
■ Maintaining rising levels of expenditure on health and education
■ Raising the level of the minimum wage
■ Keeping the UK in the European Union
■ Holding firm on emissions targets
■ Keeping up levels of international aid
■ Reforming parliament (though they may disagree on methods)
■ Granting more autonomy to large cities and regions
■ Encouraging higher levels of house building

This is an impressive list and looks like the basis for a stable coalition.

Exam focus

To consolidate your knowledge of this chapter, answer the following questions:

1 Outline the main areas of political consensus in British politics.
2 Explain the main adversarial issues in British politics.
3 Outline how coalition governments are able to survive.
4 On what issues do Liberal Democrats and Conservatives agree or disagree?
5 On what grounds do Liberal Democrats agree with the Labour Party on policy?

Chapter 6

Pressure groups: have the internet and social media affected their activities?

Exam success

The up-to-date facts, examples and arguments in this chapter will help you to produce good quality answers in your AS unit tests in the following areas of the specifications:

Edexcel	AQA	OCR
Unit 1	**Unit 1**	**Unit F851**
Pressure groups	Pressure groups and protest movements	Pressure groups

Context

The activities of pressure groups in the UK have been considerably affected by two main developments:

1 the decline in the importance of political parties, particularly *mass* parties
2 the growth in the importance of the internet and social media, which has been accompanied by a decline in the influence of the traditional media – the published press, TV and radio – in terms of information and opinion.

These changes have created both opportunities and problems for pressure groups. The decline in political parties can be measured largely in terms of falling membership. In the early 1980s about two million people were members of one of the three main parties. Today, though exact figures are difficult to come by, the number is probably well below 400,000. This has meant that pressure groups have been able to exploit the vacuum and recruit members and supporters who would formerly have pursued their political beliefs through parties.

Arguably today, however, it is the growing importance of the internet and social media that is mainly driving the changes in the ways that pressure groups operate. Indeed, as we shall see below, it may be better to speak of **movements** than **groups** as the internet allows people to participate and follow without necessarily becoming formal members of any organisation.

Social movements

Social movements, sometimes called **new social movements** have, to some extent, replaced formal pressure groups as channels of influence and as means by which people can participate in political issues. Increasingly we refer to **movements** rather than **groups**. The more formal pressure groups have often become elements of these movements, without necessarily dominating them.

The relevance of the internet and social media here is that they have created opportunities for movements to flourish without recruiting formal memberships. This has occurred in a number of ways:

- There is more open communication among those who are interested in an issue. By interrogating the web and social media everyone can become informed about an issue, learning facts and absorbing opinions. This is occurring through blogs, Twitter and the other forms of social media that have grown up, including YouTube, Meetup, IRC (Internet Relay Chat) and Facebook.
- Social networks have made it possible to organise events quickly and on a large scale. These include demonstrations, protest camps, boycotts and acts of civil disobedience.
- Organising such movements is relatively cheap. Traditionally, pressure groups needed extensive resources, usually gathered through donations and membership fees, to be able to campaign. The internet and social media are largely free, so even small organisations can mount large campaigns involving many thousands of supporters.
- One perspective on these changes is that pressure groups represented a 'professional approach' to the mobilisation of influence. Social movements using the internet can be essentially 'amateur' organisations.
- We can also say that the politics of pressure is becoming more democratised. Though it has always been claimed that pressure groups are more democratic than parties, in terms of dispersing influence more widely, social movements are even more democratic, allowing for mass participation and a completely open, free market in opinion.

Table 6.1 shows examples of these social movements from recent times, including those formal pressure groups that have become involved with them and which, to some extent, may have been replaced.

The movements shown in the table all rely heavily on social media to publicise their issues, recruit adherents, organise events and demonstrations and to demonstrate to decision makers the strength of their support.

Table 6.1 Social movements and pressure groups

Movement	Aims and policies	Examples of associated pressure groups
The environment movement	Cluster of issues, including emissions control, global warming, biodiversity, sustainability.	Friends of the Earth Greenpeace Waste Watch National Society for Clean Air
The Occupy movement	Campaigning against the excesses of the banking system, the 'immoral' behaviour of multinationals, excessive corporate pay, tax evasion and avoidance.	UK Uncut (anti-austerity) Consumers' Association
Anti-globalisation movement	Counter the activities of multinational organisations which lead to low wages in poor countries, exploitation of child labour, environmental problems, etc.	Greenpeace Friends of the Earth Global Citizens' Movement
Anti-fracking movement	Opposing plans to extract gas by the controversial fracking method.	Friends of the Earth Frack Off Various local campaign groups

Digital democracy

This term refers to the ways in which the democratic process is increasingly being conducted through the internet. The main features of digital democracy are:

- The internet has created a free forum for comment and opinion.
- It also provides a ready means by which information can be found and disseminated. This means that it is more difficult for public bodies, parties or pressure groups to manipulate information for their own ends. It is argued that open access to the internet renders it more democratic.
- It is now common for both individuals and pressure groups to organise campaigns through the internet. Methods include the gathering of e-petitions, write-in campaigns to ministers and MPs, together with events designed to demonstrate the scale of public support.

There are now a number of sites that help both individuals and pressure groups to organise campaigns. The best known are 38 Degrees (UK-based) and Avaaz (global). Here are some examples of campaigns run by these two in 2014:

Avaaz

- whale conservation
- fighting global tax evasion
- banning bee-killing pesticides
- stopping internet censorship

38 Degrees

- campaigning against puppy farming
- opposing the sale of arms to Israel
- opposing zero-hours contracts

These sites are a threat to traditional pressure groups. In particular they are able to concentrate on *specific* issues in a way that pressure groups do not. They can also organise very precise campaigns and mobilise support for them.

Pressure group response to the growth of social media

Despite the rise of social movements, pressure groups remain the most important way in which people can influence government at all levels. It is still true that **insider** status can be highly effective. Large, wealthy pressure groups can also still mount major campaigns. It is also true that government prefers to deal with what it considers to be 'legitimate' channels of communication.

The real influence of the internet has been seen, therefore, with **outsider** groups. Outsider groups are those that do not have special links with decision makers. They tend to concern themselves with issues, rather than particular sections of the community, and their main weapon is usually public opinion. Outsider groups seek to achieve the following:

- To mobilise public support about an issue.
- To organise various kinds of demonstrations of the size of that support.
- To persuade government and other decision makers that support is so widespread that it will be in their own interests to listen to their demands.

Votes motivate accountable decision makers. Pressure groups that can persuade them that the issue they are campaigning for will influence how people vote will be persuasive.

The internet and social media can be effectively used by these pressure groups in a number of ways:

- They can register large numbers of supporters efficiently and quickly.
- They can publicise issues widely through social media.
- They can inform their supporters about the action they are taking.
- They can gather support by ensuring that issues trend on networks like Twitter.
- They can organise e-petitions either on public sites or on the government's Downing Street site.

The table below shows examples of recent social media campaigns conducted by various groups:

Table 6.2 Internet and social media campaigns

Group	Issue	Methods
Hacked Off	Campaigning for tighter regulation of the press.	Use of celebrities through social media, notably Twitter and Facebook.
Trade Union movement	Campaigning against zero-hours contracts.	Support for e-petitions.
Greenpeace	Stopping Norway over-exploiting the Arctic Ocean causing environmental damage.	Blogging Twitter Facebook contacts to members. Facebook campaign to gain new members.
Taxpayers' Alliance	Reducing UK taxes.	Publishing research papers on the internet.
Plane Stupid	Arguing against airport expansion in southeast England.	Using social media to organise mass demonstrations and acts of civil disobedience.

Do these developments enhance or threaten democracy?

They enhance democracy

- There is no doubt that the internet and social media have transformed the world of popular politics. It has widened the scope for participation, bringing in people who would never have thought of joining a party or even a formal pressure group.
- The developments have helped to disperse power and influence more widely. If such pluralism is a measure of a healthy democracy then it has had a positive effect. One of the problems of pressure group politics has been that it has been *asymmetric*, that is, different groups have had different degrees of influence. Naturally larger and wealthier groups have had the most influence, while a number of small but well-resourced groups have wielded a disproportionate amount of power. The internet has helped to equalise the influence of different groups, largely because it is possible to campaign even with meagre funding.
- A democratic society depends upon a well-informed electorate. Both the internet and social media have helped to disseminate information and opinion more widely.
- They have also opened up lines of communication between the governed and the government. Governments need to be able to gauge the strength of opinions on issues if they are to govern well and secure consent for their policies. The issue of fracking is a good example of this, as are the debates about High Speed 2, and how to increase airport capacity in the southeast of England.

They threaten democracy

- The internet is like a garden. It contains both desirable flowers and undesirable weeds, but it is not always possible to distinguish between the two. In practice this means that it is hard to know which arguments are valid and which facts are true. All participants in social media have the same credibility even though some do not deserve it. A good deal of false information on the environment, for example, has been discovered.
- It may put *too* much pressure on government so that it does not govern in a rational way, but instead operates on knee-jerk reactions.
- Social media may have caused a rise in antisocial, sometimes illegal activity by campaign movements. The Occupy movement and some animal rights groups have been accused of such widespread activities. Several years ago, when there were sharp rises in fuel prices, a social media-driven movement among motorists and road haulage companies led to widespread disobedience to the inconvenience of the public.

Summary

Social media and the internet in general have undoubtedly transformed the world of pressure group politics. It has enabled groups to campaign on **single issues** and not just in terms of generalised policy areas. It also means that campaigns can be mounted very quickly and can involve a much wider proportion of the informed population. Governments at all levels, national, regional and local, have also had to respond. The growth in the use of e-petitions, in particular, has forced decision makers to listen to public opinion. Of course, governments themselves use the internet to put across their own views and policies in an attempt to gain support for them. This has led to a much more extensive **two-way dialogue** between government and the governed. It has also removed the inbuilt advantage that larger and wealthier groups have enjoyed over smaller, weaker and poorer groups. This means that influence in UK democracy is now more widely dispersed.

Because it is easier to mount popular campaigns using social media and the internet it has increased the use of **direct action,** but it has also opened the door to more **civil disobedience** and illegal activities so the picture remains a mixed one. Having said this, pressure groups continue to operate in traditional ways, notably insider groups which are mostly sectional. They still seek direct links with decision makers, lobbying of parliament and mounting large-scale demonstrations, and they still promote legislation or oppose unfavourable proposals through Parliament.

Exam focus

To consolidate your knowledge of this chapter, answer the following questions:

1 What is meant by the term *digital democracy*?
2 How have social movements replaced some of the functions of pressure groups?
3 How have pressure groups used the internet to enhance their activities?
4 Does the use of social media in the politics of pressure groups enhance or threaten democracy?

Chapter 7

The cabinet reshuffle: a ruthless display of prime ministerial power?

Exam success

The up-to-date facts, examples and arguments in this chapter will help you to produce good quality answers in your AS unit tests in the following areas of the specifications:

Edexcel	AQA	OCR
Unit 2	**Unit 2**	**Unit F582**
The prime minister and cabinet	The core executive	The executive

Context

In July 2014 David Cameron reshuffled his cabinet. This came as no surprise. It is normal for a prime minister to make regular changes to his ministerial team and this is particularly true one year before a general election. What was unusual on this occasion was the scale of the changes and the way in which the prime minister appeared to have signalled a change in direction as a result of his new appointments, dismissals and promotions.

Commentators were divided over the motives behind the changes. Some argued it was a sign that the prime minister was starting to panic as the election approached and his party still lagged behind Labour in the opinion polls. Others suggested it was an attempt to head off the growing challenge to his leadership of the eurosceptic wing of the party. A third perspective concentrated on the fact that several new appointments were of young female members. This was therefore to answer criticisms that too many members of the government were from a similar background – male, white, middle-aged and public school educated. A fourth explanation is especially examined in this chapter. This is that Cameron wished to exert his authority over both the government and his party. By changing his frontbench team he demonstrated his authority. This was especially thought to be true in relation to the demotion of Michael Gove, a potential leadership rival.

The reshuffle also took place in the context of the rise of UKIP, demonstrated by their powerful performance in the 2014 European parliament elections. The overall impression was that there was a shift to the right in the party leadership, notably over such issues as Europe and immigration.

Prime ministerial patronage

We should remind ourselves that the UK prime minister has complete power of patronage over his ministerial team, both cabinet ministers and other junior posts. He does not need to seek the approval of any other body. This power is a major source of his authority. Leading members of the party need to show loyalty to him to have a chance of promotion. Similarly, once appointed he can exercise discipline as he can always threaten an individual with dismissal if they are too rebellious.

But this does not mean that the prime minister has a completely free hand. He must take certain factors into consideration, for example:

- He may wish to keep rivals at bay by promoting them. The doctrine of collective responsibility means that ministers must toe the party line, resign or face dismissal. This can have the effect of silencing critics.
- Prime ministers have political debts to pay. Those who have supported him or her regularly need rewarding. This often entails granting them a post in the government.
- The prime minister needs to be aware of public opinion. His government team needs to contain individuals who are popular, both with the public and with the party.
- He must decide whether he wants a 'balanced' cabinet, where all factions of his party are represented, or a team containing all his closer allies, to give it a sense of unity.
- Under coalition, and this only apples to coalition government, he must also grant an agreed number of posts to the junior partner, in this case the Liberal Democrats. When a vacancy arises because a Liberal Democrat leaves the government, he or she must be replaced by a Liberal Democrat. Who that replacement is, is a matter of discussion and agreement between the leaders of the two coalition parties, i.e. the prime minister and deputy prime minister.

Individual factors in choosing ministers

There are a number of reasons why an individual may be appointed to a ministerial post, inside or outside the cabinet. The main ones are:

- An individual may have a considerable following in the party, or may represent a particular faction that needs to be represented in the government.
- Someone may have outstanding personal qualities.
- If an MP shows a particular skill in debating and handling affairs in the House of Commons he or she is more likely to make a success of ministerial office.
- The prime minister may have a debt of loyalty to repay. This is often when he or she was supported by that person in the past in a leadership contest.
- The prime minister may offer a dissident a cabinet post to stifle him or her. The principle of collective responsibility prevents cabinet ministers opposing official policy.
- Occasionally, though not compulsorily, an individual may have a great deal of specific experience and expertise to bring to ministerial office.

The 2014 reshuffle

The table below shows the ins, outs and transfers in the new cabinet, together with some reasons why they were made:

Table 7.1 The 2014 cabinet reshuffle

New members		
Minister	**Post**	**Reason**
Michael Fallon	Defence Secretary	Specialist in crisis management. Response to Middle East problems.
Nicky Morgan	Education Secretary	On the right of the party. As a woman she improves the gender balance of the cabinet.
Liz Truss	Environment, Food and Rural Affairs	In line with government environment policy. Improves cabinet gender balance. Good media image.
Stephen Crabb	Welsh Secretary	Cameron loyalist.

Transfers			
Minister	**From**	**To**	**Reason**
William Hague	Foreign Secretary	Leader of the House	Hague will retire from politics after 2015, so he was moved to a less important post.
Philip Hammond	Defence Secretary	Foreign Secretary	Promotion for a leading eurosceptic. Response to rise of UKIP.

Removed from cabinet		
Minister	**Former post**	**Reason**
Michael Gove	Education Secretary	Unpopular in the country and teaching profession. Has made too many enemies in government. A possible leadership rival to Cameron.
Andrew Lansley	Leader of the House of Commons	Poor media image. Unpopular in the party.
Owen Paterson	Environment, Food and Rural Affairs	A climate change sceptic so defies government policy. Poor ministerial record.
David Jones	Welsh Secretary	Poor ministerial record.
Kenneth Clarke*	Minister without portfolio (no department)	*Technically he resigned, but may have been forced out. Considered too liberal and too pro-European.
David Willetts	Universities Minister	Retiring from politics.

Other non-cabinet appointments included:

Michael Gove was dismissed as Education Secretary and appointed government **Chief Whip**. The Chief Whip often attends cabinet meetings but is not a member. This removes him from the central policy-making machine of the government and so removes an important rival to Cameron's authority.

Esther McVeigh became a **junior employment minister**. She improves the government's gender balance. She had a career in the media before politics and so will improve the party image.

Baroness Stowell was promoted to **Leader of the House of Lords**. Another woman to improve the gender balance and has a good media image.

Priti Patel became a **junior treasury minister**. Not only a woman, but also from an ethnic minority so improves inclusivity image of government. A prominent right-winger, she also shifts the political balance of the government in the face of the UKIP challenge.

What might be the effects of the changes on government?

There has been some re-balancing of the cabinet towards women. However, the cabinet itself is still male-dominated. It will also be a slightly younger government. However, the charge that Cameron's government is still dominated by privately educated men, largely from the south of England, remains. Certainly Eton remains over-represented.

Politically the government has shifted a little to the right. This is mainly in terms of attitudes to Britain's relationship to the EU (including migration from within the EU), immigration and law and order. This will help the Conservatives in their conflict with UKIP.

There has been some progress towards making the government more ethnically diverse. However ethnic minorities are still under-represented and the position was made worse a month after the reshuffle, when Baroness Warsi, a leading Muslim, resigned over the government's position in the Israeli–Arab conflict in Gaza during the summer.

Why did Cameron reshuffle his pack?

There are three main theories about the reasons behind this reshuffle:

1 This was a pre-election clear-out. Cameron wanted a team that would look better to the electorate, younger, fresher, more diverse and with good media images. He removed unpopular ministers such as Michael Gove and Andrew Lansley, and promoted individuals who would attract more votes, such as Esther McVeigh and Liz Truss.

2 This was largely about the challenge of UKIP. Cameron wanted a government that would be more euro-sceptic and more right-wing generally.

3 That it was an attempt by David Cameron to shore up his waning authority. By asserting his patronage power he wanted to appear to be a strong leader at a time when there were whispers that he was too weak. He cleared out potential opponents and promoted a number of loyalists.

There is probably truth within all these ideas. Certainly it is normal that a prime minister makes one last remodelling of the government before a general election, so perhaps we should not read too much into this.

Summary

This was one of the largest government reshuffles in recent British history. It once again demonstrates the importance of prime ministerial patronage. By maintaining complete personal control over ministerial appointments, a prime minister is able to keep control of the government and underpin his power. Was this a demonstration of the ruthless power of a leader? In a sense it was, but whether it was actually 'ruthless' is questionable. Had Cameron gone too far he might have created a large body of opposition within his party so he had to tread carefully.

Exam focus

To consolidate your knowledge of this chapter, answer the following questions:

1 What factors does a prime minister take into account when appointing ministers?
2 Why do prime ministers regularly reshuffle their cabinets?
3 Explain the importance of prime ministerial patronage.
4 What qualities does a government minister need to have?
5 Under what circumstances do ministers sometimes lose their jobs?
6 Are ministers too homogeneous today?

Chapter 8

Prime Minister's Questions: more than just a pantomime?

Exam success

The up-to-date facts, examples and arguments in this chapter will help you to produce good quality answers in your AS unit tests in the following areas of the specifications:

Edexcel	AQA	OCR
Unit 2	**Unit 2**	**Unit F582**
Parliament	Parliament	The legislature

Context

It is a fundamental principle of modern democratic government that representatives should be accountable. As this can only occur *directly* at elections, accountability has largely to be achieved through Parliament. The prime minister himself is no exception to this. He is questioned regularly by the Parliamentary Liaison Committee of the House of Commons, but this receives relatively little publicity. Virtually every Wednesday, therefore, the prime minister is subjected to half an hour of questioning by the leader of the opposition and various backbench MPs, both from his own party and the opposition.

In the last few decades this event has received increasing amounts of publicity. It is, indeed, virtually the only parliamentary event that receives significant coverage on TV and radio. However, there has also been increasing concern that Prime Minister's Questions (PMQs) has become little more than a 'circus' or a 'pantomime' which now has little to do with true accountability. Yet, repeated attempts to change the conduct of the leaders and the MPs have failed.

The televising of Parliament

After several unsuccessful attempts to introduce the televising of Parliament, supporters were finally rewarded in November 1989 when the first televised debates arrived. Prime Minister Margaret Thatcher had opposed the move, suggesting it would bring Parliament into disrepute. She was afraid that some examples of 'bad behaviour' might be seen clearly by the public. Supporters, however, were clear that it was a vital development for British democracy.

In the years since 1989 the main aspect of Parliament that has been shown on TV has been Prime Minister's Questions. Originally the session was held twice a week, but under Tony Blair it was reduced to a single half-hour session every Wednesday. Many critics have suggested that Mrs Thatcher's fears have come true. Despite repeated attempts, notably by the Speaker of the Commons, behaviour at PMQs has steadily deteriorated.

Criticism of PMQs grows

On 6 July 2010 the House of Commons speaker, John Bercow, made a speech to the Centre for Parliamentary Studies. In the course of this speech he reopened the debate about the problems of Prime Minister's Questions. He said this:

> Prime Minister's Questions is the shop window of the House of Commons. The media coverage of that thirty minute slot dominates all other proceedings in Parliament during the rest of the week. If the country comes to an adverse conclusion about the House because of what it witnesses in those exchanges, then the noble work of a dozen Select Committees will pale into insignificance by comparison. If we are serious about enhancing the standing of the House in the eyes of those whom we serve then we cannot ignore the seriously impaired impression which PMQs has been and is leaving on the electorate.

> There will be some of my colleagues who I expect, very sincerely, to disagree with me. They argue that PMQs is splendid theatre, that it is secretly loved by those watching on television and that it is even therapeutic for parliamentarians to let their lungs loose on a weekly basis. I have to say that I find this argument utterly unconvincing. On the basis of its logic, bear-baiting and cock-fighting would still be legal activities.

Source: Centre for Parliamentary Studies

In April 2014 Bercow renewed his attack in a press interview. He was particularly concerned that women would be put off attending the chamber or even entering politics if they have to put up with what he saw as 'male-dominated' childish behaviour. He said this:

> I think it is a big deal. I think it is a real problem. A number of seasoned parliamentarians, who are not shrinking violets, not delicate creatures at all, are saying, 'This is so bad that I am not going to take part, I am not going to come along, I feel embarrassed by it.' People with a lot to contribute are reluctant to engage because they think that the histrionics and cacophony of noise are so damaging as to cause them to look elsewhere. But I'm sorry if some of those people are lost to the chamber because they think, 'I'm not going to take part in that atmosphere'.

Labour leader, Ed Miliband, supported Bercow:

> I think it subtracts from the reputation of politics. I think lots of previous leaders, not just of the Labour party, but of the Conservative party would say that too. It's easy to say it's a problem, it's harder to change it, but I'm totally up for finding ways to change it...We should endeavour to be proud of the show we put on for the country, not giving people a sense that their kids behave better than we do.

Liberal Democrat leader, Nick Clegg, has joined Miliband in this criticism. The Conservatives, on the other hand, have been largely silent on the issue.

How Prime Minister's Questions has been misused

PMQs has always existed in order to force the prime minister and the government to be accountable to Parliament. It is meant to throw a spotlight on government actions and policy, force the government to justify its actions and give MPs the opportunity to express criticisms. However, in recent times it has been 'misused' in a number of ways:

Highlighting successful government policy

PMQs is often used as a way of highlighting a successful government policy. This is not what it is intended for, but it is often used in this way. Here a question has probably been 'planted' (that is, a government MP has been asked to put a question so that the prime minister can mention a success):

> **Mrs Cheryl Gillan (Chesham and Amersham) (Con):** People with autism have specific social and communications needs which can cause distress and misunderstanding, particularly when they are admitted to hospital for routine or emergency treatment. Will the prime minister join me in congratulating Baroness Angela Browning and the National Autistic Society, who tomorrow will launch the new hospital passport for people with autism? That will make a great difference to many people's lives in this country.
>
> **The Prime Minister:** I thank my Right Hon. Friend for raising this important issue. Baroness Browning has worked very hard on this issue over many years in both Houses, as has my Right Hon. Friend. The Autism Act 2009 is making a huge difference to the way that we help young people with these conditions. I join her in making sure that these services are properly put together.
>
> Source: Hansard, 16 July 2014

MPs publicise their own achievements in their constituencies

Here is an example of an MP using PMQs to publicise some of his own work in his constituency:

> **Andrew Jones (Harrogate and Knaresborough) (Con):** Later this year, North Yorkshire will become the best connected county in terms of superfast broadband, which is hugely helpful for our growing hospitality and tourism industry, which already provides thousands of jobs in my Harrogate and Knaresborough constituency and received a wonderful boost from the recent visit of the Tour de France. Does my Right Hon. Friend agree that rolling out superfast broadband is a great boost for jobs in all sectors, not just hospitality, and will help to build upon the wonderful economic legacy of the Tour de France?
>
> **The Prime Minister:** I thank my Hon. Friend for the warm welcome that he and people in Harrogate gave me during the stage of the Tour de France, marred

only by Mark Cavendish's tragic accident. It was an extraordinary event and showed his constituency and the whole of Yorkshire in their best light. He is quite right about the importance of superfast broadband. We are putting £790 million into superfast broadband access. We have half a million UK premises connected already and around 400,000 new premises are being upgraded every week. Everyone in the House has a duty to get out there to help to advertise what is happening with broadband and to encourage take-up rates.

Source: Hansard, 16 July 2014

Note that this MP also takes the opportunity to ingratiate himself with the prime minister.

Using PMQs to criticise the opposition

Here is an example of the prime minister ignoring a specific question and, instead, having a snipe at the opposition.

Fiona O'Donnell (East Lothian) (Lab): Returning to the issue of taxes and the wealthy, when will the Prime Minister keep his promise and publish his tax return?

The Prime Minister: On the subject of taxes and middle income people, when will we get an answer from Labour about what the deputy Leader of the party meant when she said – let me repeat it again for the record:

'I think people on middle incomes should contribute more through their taxes'?

As we go into the summer, there is one party in this House with a big tax problem, and I am looking at it.

Source: Hansard, 16 July 2014

MPs use it as an opportunity to behave in a rowdy fashion

Here the speaker has to reprimand a Labour backbench MP, Fiona Mactaggart, for unacceptable behaviour. She was continually heckling the prime minister. The speaker's comments are certainly sarcastic in nature! Note how the prime minister uses the exchange to jibe at the opposition party.

Mr Speaker: Order. There is far too much noise in the Chamber. Ms Mactaggart, you are an illustrious product of the Cheltenham Ladies' College. I cannot believe they taught you there to behave like that.

The Prime Minister: You are right, Mr Speaker, that there is a lot of history in this shouting, because of course in the past with all these privatisations we had the shouting of the Kinnocks, the shouting of the Prescotts and the shouting of the Straws. Over Easter, I was looking at Labour's candidates and I saw that son of Kinnock is coming here, son of Straw wants to get here and son of Prescott wants to come here. It is the same families with the same message – it is literally the same old Labour. That is what is happening.

Source: Hansard, 30 April 2014

The opposition leader using PMQs to publicise his own party's policies

Here Ed Miliband takes the opportunity to point out that the Labour Party is proposing to freeze energy prices if it gets into power, a policy that has proved to be very popular.

> **Edward Miliband:** The Right Hon. Gentleman is not the Prime Minister at all; he is the PR man for the energy companies – that is what he is. Bills are rising and what is clear is that his argument against a freeze has been totally demolished today. A price freeze for households and businesses is feasible, workable and will happen under a Labour Government.
>
> Source: Hansard, 26 March 2014

An assessment of PMQs

Despite all the criticism, Prime Minister's Questions does have its supporters. The table below offers a balanced assessment of PMQs:

Table 8.1 Prime Minister's Questions – arguments for and against

Arguments For	Arguments Against
• It is a crucial way of making government accountable. • It makes popular viewing and so engages people in politics. • It is the only occasion when backbench MPs are able to question the prime minister directly. • Some argue it demonstrates how vibrant and confrontational British politics can be.	• It has been so severely misused that it has ceased to perform its correct function of making government accountable. • Behaviour has become so poor that it is putting people off politics. • It presents a poor view of British democracy to the outside world. • Some voters may be excessively influenced by how party leaders perform at PMQs.

Certainly PMQs is in marked contrast to the apparently 'dull' politics seen in many other European democracies. However, the lack of rational debate can be seen as a criticism. Above all, the danger is that a party leader who may be admirable in many ways, could be seen as weak because of a poor showing at PMQs. It has become something of a showcase for politics, but should not be mistaken for 'genuine' political debate.

Summary

It used to be accepted that Prime Minister's Questions was an important way in which government is made accountable in the UK. The picture today, however, is very different. PMQs has become little more than a media event. Its role seems to be to allow the electorate to make judgements about the merits of the party leaders in debating, and little more. The fact that all attempts to reform it have failed suggests that both the main parties are content to leave it in place.

On the other hand, in an age when there is a great deal of disengagement with politics, anything that can capture people's interest may be useful. Parliamentary politics is, on the whole, dull. PMQs does help to make politics more exciting.

Exam focus

To consolidate your knowledge of this chapter, answer the following questions:

1 How does Parliament make government accountable?
2 Assess the importance of Prime Minister's Questions.
3 Why is Prime Minister's Questions often described as ineffective?

Ed Miliband: the wrong brother?

Exam success

The up-to-date facts, examples and arguments in this chapter will help you to produce good quality answers in your AS unit tests in the following areas of the specifications:

Edexcel	AQA	OCR
Unit 1	**Unit 1**	**Unit F851**
Party policies and ideas	Political parties	Political parties

Context

When Labour leader Gordon Brown resigned in 2010, shortly after losing the general election of that year and failing to form a coalition government, the party held a leadership contest. It was fully expected that David Miliband, the older son of radical socialist historian and philosopher Ralph Miliband, would win the contest. Apart from being older and slightly more experienced than his brother Ed, David was undoubtedly the first choice of Labour MPs and polls suggested that the public agreed with this verdict.

That David did not win was largely the result of the way in which Labour elects its leader. This system is described below. What followed had some of the elements of a Greek tragedy. The younger brother, Ed, won the contest at the last gasp. It had been expected that Ed might stand down in favour of his brother (just as Gordon Brown had withdrawn from the leadership contest of 1992 in favour of Tony Blair), but he did not. As a result David left politics and was seen as a disillusioned figure, forced out of mainstream politics. It is not now well known how relations are between the brothers.

The years since the 2010 election have seen Ed Miliband lagging behind his rival, David Cameron, in opinion polls. Even though Labour is more popular than the Conservative Party consistently in the polls, Ed remains relatively unpopular. This chapter examines how this situation came about.

Ralph Miliband

Ralph Miliband (1924–94) was a Marxist historian and theorist, the son of Jewish, Polish parents, who settled in Britain after the Second World War. He joined the Labour Party but became one of its severest internal critics from the 1960s onwards. In his historical study, *Parliamentary Socialism*, written in 1961, he argued that the Labour Party was not radical enough, having sacrificed many of its socialist principles for the sake of trying to win power. He also asserted that the conflict between the two great classes – working and middle – was still a fundamental feature of modern society. His analysis was similar to that of Marx himself who argued that capitalism could not solve the conflict as the interests of the two classes were irreconcilable. Labour, he complained, had made too many compromises.

Ralph Miliband also analysed the true nature of capitalist power in modern democratic society. In *The State in Capitalist Society* (1969) he argued that liberal democracy was an illusion and that the permanent apparatus of the state remained in the hands of the leadership of the bourgeois class.

As the Labour Party gradually moved further away from its socialist roots, Miliband senior grew increasingly critical, but he also became marginalised on the left of British politics. By the time of his death in 1994 his views were seen as well outside the spectrum of conventional politics. At the same time, the end of the Cold War and the demise of the Soviet Union had led to a belief that Marxist ideas had finally become irrelevant. By the time his two sons were adults, Ralph Miliband had ceased to have any serious influence on left-wing politics in Britain.

Clearly Ralph must have been a great influence on his two sons, David and Ed. However, by the time they were entering politics, at the end of their father's life, Labour Party politics had moved on. The left wing of the party had been eclipsed by the emergence of New Labour in the early 1990s. It was not surprising, therefore, that the two brothers should harbour much more moderate views than their father. Although there have been some claims that the radicalism of the father is a disadvantage to the sons (some even claiming that Ralph was unpatriotic), both have, on the whole, succeeded in staying faithful to the memory of their father without being 'tainted' by his Marxist ideals.

How Labour elects its leader

It is extremely important to understand how the election of a Labour leader works because it explains how it was that Ed Miliband, the less considered candidate, was able to win.

Stage 1: nominations

To enter the election, a candidate must be nominated by at least 12.5% of the party's MPs in the House of Commons. In 2010 that number was 33. Five candidates achieved this minimum number. They were as follows:

Table 9.1 Labour leadership nominations, 2010

Candidate	Nominations	% of Labour MPs
David Miliband	81	31.5
Ed Miliband	63	24.5
Diane Abbott	33	12.8
Andy Burnham	33	12.8
Ed Balls	33	12.8

It seemed clear that there were only two serious candidates – the Miliband brothers. It was also clear that, within the Labour parliamentary party, David was a clear favourite. Some expected Ed to stand down at this stage in favour of David. Assuming he asked his supporters to vote for David, the contest would have been effectively over. But this did not happen and the contest went through to stage 2.

Stage 2: the first ballot

All five candidates were entitled to enter the ballot and all five did so. For the purpose of the election the party is divided into three sections:

Section 1   Labour MPs and Members of the European Parliament

Section 2   Members of trade unions and other connected (affiliated) societies such as the Fabian Society and the Co-operative movement

Section 3   Labour Party members outside parliament

Each section carries equal weight. The votes in each are converted into percentages, the three percentages are then added to give an overall figure for each candidate. If any candidate ends with a total above 50% he or she will be elected leader at this stage. Failing that, the candidate with the lowest level of support has to drop out and a second ballot is held. This process continues until there are only two candidates left in the contest.

The result of the first ballot was as follows:

Table 9.2 Labour leadership election, 2010: first ballot

Candidate	MPs/MEPs %	Trade Union and Societies %	Members %	Total %
David Miliband	13.9	9.2	14.7	37.8
Ed Miliband	10.5	13.8	10.0	34.3
Ed Balls	5.0	3.4	3.4	11.8
Andy Burnham	3.0	2.8	2.9	8.7
Diane Abbott	0.9	4.1	2.5	7.4

Diane Abbott was bottom of the first ballot and had to drop out.

After the first ballot two features become clear. First, that only two candidates really mattered – the Miliband brothers. They were too far ahead for any of the others to hope for victory. Secondly, David was more popular among MPs and ordinary party members, but Ed won the contest among trade union members. Despite the fact that David had won in two of the three sections, Ed did not stand down.

The next question was where would the votes for Diane Abbott, the eliminated candidate, go?

Stage 3: the second ballot

Table 9.3 Labour leadership election, 2010: second ballot

Candidate	MPs/MEPs %	Trade Union and Societies %	Members %	Total %
David Miliband	14.0	9.8	15.1	38.9
Ed Miliband	11.1	15.2	11.1	37.5
Ed Balls	5.2	4.2	3.8	13.2
Andy Burnham	3.0	4.1	3.3	10.4

Little was changed by this ballot. Andy Burnham dropped out, but Ed Balls fought on despite his cause being hopeless. The relative positions of the two brothers changed little though Ed gained a slight advantage because most of Diane Abbott's support (she was the most left wing of the candidates) went to Ed.

Stage 4: the third ballot

Table 9.4 Labour leadership election, 2010: third ballot

Candidate	MPs/MEPs %	Trade Union and Societies %	Members %	Total %
David Miliband	15.8	10.9	16.1	42.8
Ed Miliband	12.1	16.7	12.4	41.2
Ed Balls	5.4	5.8	4.8	16.0

Ed Balls now had to drop out. At the next stage, with only two candidates, one was bound to win outright.

Stage 5: the fourth ballot

Table 9.5 Labour leadership election, 2010: fourth ballot

Candidate	MPs/MEPs %	Trade Union and Societies %	Members %	Total %
Ed Miliband	15.5	19.9	15.2	50.7
David Miliband	17.8	13.4	18.1	49.3

The result was dramatic. David Miliband was still the preferred choice of members and MPs and MEPs, but Ed won because the trade unions and societies supported him so decisively.

Was this a 'wrong result'?

It could be seen as faulty in two main senses:

1 David Miliband won the vote from two sections of the party. Ed only won one section.

2 David was more popular in Parliament. It was going to be difficult for Ed to hold the party together. He was going to have to lead in Parliament when he was not the most popular choice of MPs.

Was it a 'right result'?

The result was right in the sense that, under the rules of the party, Ed won. Labour is seen as a 'federal' party. In order to lead, therefore, it is argued that a candidate must be able to unite all three sections. A leader who cannot command the support of the trade unions is seen as especially vulnerable.

Policy differences

We must also consider whether Ed is the 'wrong' brother for Labour in terms of their respective policies. In general terms Ed has been seen as more left wing than his brother and many see this as a disadvantage. It is often said that elections are won from the centre. David Miliband was seen as sitting in that centre. This has become especially important as the Conservative Party, in the face of the UKIP challenge, has been moving to the right, while Liberal Democrat support has collapsed. This has left the centre ground more available.

The differences in the policy positions of the brothers are quite subtle and it has to be remembered that David might have changed his policy had he been leader in the four years between 2010 and 2014. It also must be said that there are no dramatic differences; it is more a case of different emphases. A comparison remains, therefore, rather speculative. The effects of policy differences may also be exaggerated. The general 'image' of the two may well be more significant. Some general points are:

Table 9.6 David and Ed Miliband: policy comparison

Issue	Ed Miliband	David Miliband
General political stance	Just left of centre. Seen as anti-Blair.	Centre. Seen as a Blairite.
Foreign policy	Less interventionist.	More interventionist.
Economic policy	More emphasis on economic growth than financial stability.	More emphasis on financial stability.
Taxation	Proposing more redistribution of the tax burden towards the wealthy.	Less radical on shifting the tax burden.
Welfare state	More suspicious of private sector involvement.	More amenable to private sector involvement.
Education	More egalitarian attitude to education.	More conservative on education policy.
Areas of general agreement between the two		

- Attitude to the European Union.
- The issue of devolution and constitutional change.
- Policy towards trade unions and the unions' links with Labour.
- Similar views on transport infrastructure.
- Similar on environmental issues.

Non-political differences

As we can see, these differences are not very significant. It may well be that there are other factors to be taken into consideration when comparing them:

- David has more senior political experience.
- David enjoys a better media image and is said to have more charisma.
- As a former Foreign Secretary and currently CEO of an international NGO, David has a higher profile abroad.
- Ed is seen as a little 'geekish' and awkward. David has a more sophisticated image.
- Ed does display more political passion than his older brother.
- Ed is seen as closer to the 'grass roots' of the Labour Party, notably trade union members.

Opinion poll evidence

The differences in image and personality are reflected in opinion poll surveys concerning the two men.

A YouGov poll in September 2014 asked a sample of voters the following question:

> If you woke up the day after the next election to find that Ed Miliband had become prime minister, would you be...?

The respondents gave the following answers:

Delighted	9%
Mildly pleased	9%
Just relieved the Conservatives were out	21%
Mildly concerned	21%
Angry	4%
Depressed	32%
None/Don't know	4%

Source: YouGov

This is far from a ringing endorsement! If we add up all those who would feel concerned or negative about Ed Miliband being prime minister we find that 61% would be unhappy to a greater or lesser extent. However, if we look at the opinion poll ratings for the parties as a whole at about the same time, we find that about 65% of respondents would not be intending to vote Labour. In other words Ed Miliband was not really lagging behind his party's rating in the polls. Of course we must then ask how well Ed Miliband is doing against David Cameron and how well Labour would do if someone else were the party leader.

At the same time as the Miliband poll, respondents were asked about David Cameron. In terms of the three positive answers, Cameron only beat Ed Miliband

by 42% to 39%. In terms of how many would be 'depressed' if one or the other became prime minister, fewer used the term for Ed than for Cameron, though only by 33% to 32%. In other words, Miliband is doing poorly, but so is everyone else. There is a general disillusionment with Westminster politics so most leaders tend to poll badly.

In June 2014 YouGov carried out a poll to compare David with Ed Miliband as labour leaders.

Respondents were asked which party they would support with different leaders. The results came out thus:

Preferences for leadership between Ed Miliband and Cameron were:

David Cameron: 35%

Ed Miliband: 23%

But when Cameron is compared with David, the results show:

David Cameron: 23%

David Miliband: 35%

The position is exactly reversed. However we look at these figures, the polls suggest David Miliband would be preferred by voters to Ed and would be more likely to see Labour through to victory in 2015. Perhaps Labour did choose the wrong Miliband. A deeper look is needed, though, before we reach a final conclusion.

Summary

Until recent times, i.e. 10–20 years ago, the two larger parties both saw their leadership in terms of *parliamentary leadership*. In other words, the main quality of a leader was seen as their ability to unite the MPs in the parliamentary party. When this was so it was logical that the election for the leader should be held among parliamentary representatives. Now, however, it is recognised that a party leader should also be popular with the general public as well as having a strong media image. It is also essential that a leader is supported by the wider party, its grass roots members. These are the activists, the people who will campaign for the party on the ground and get people out to vote. For those reasons the leadership elections in all three main parties involve *all* party members in one way or another.

When Ed Miliband beat David to the Labour leadership in 2010, each of them appealed to different constituencies, as follows:

David

■ MPs and MEPs
■ General public
■ Media
■ Ordinary members

Ed

- Trade unionists
- Party activists

This created a clear problem. In some ways *neither* was an ideal candidate because their appeal was not wide enough. David would probably have created a more united party and would be popular with the media, but Ed does appeal to those party members who do most work for the party.

It seems unlikely that Labour will now change its leader, so close to the next general election. This is despite Ed's major gaffe at the Labour Party annual conference in September 2014 when his attempt to deliver a detailed speech without notes came adrift. He forgot to refer to key policy areas – the economy and immigration. He came in for widespread criticism, both inside and outside his own party. We must also remember, however, that David Miliband has not been involved directly in UK politics for the past four years. He is also no longer an MP. The most likely scenario which could bring David back would be a Labour defeat and an Ed Miliband resignation which would surely follow. As things stand, though, Labour remain favourites to win in 2015 so Ed may survive. His relative lack of popularity may not matter after all.

Exam focus

To consolidate your knowledge of this chapter, answer the following questions:

1 Critically examine how the Labour Party elects leaders.
2 Distinguish between the centre and left of centre in the Labour Party.
3 How important is political leadership to the parties?

Chapter 10

Briefings

This chapter will bring you up to date with some recent political developments and demonstrate how they are relevant to your studies in government and politics.

Political parties: UKIP on the march

By-elections show how much progress the party has made

The UK Independence Party (UKIP) made great electoral progress in three by-elections in the autumn of 2014. Two of the by-elections were triggered by defections from the Conservative Party to UKIP. The results of the three elections are shown below:

Table 10.1 Clacton by-election results

Candidate	Party	Votes	% of vote	% change since 2010
Carswell	UKIP	21,113	60.1	N/A*
Watling	Conservative	8,709	24.8	−28.4
Young	Labour	3,957	11.3	−13.8
Southall	Green	688	1.9	+0.7
Graham	Liberal Democrat	483	1.4	−11.5
Others	Others	183	0.5	N/A*

*There were no UKIP or minor party candidates in 2010.

This result was not a great surprise. Carswell is a popular local MP and UKIP had been gaining support there for some time. Some suggested that Carswell had defected largely because he believed that, if he remained a Conservative candidate, he would lose to UKIP so he was bowing to the inevitable. Though expected, it was still a huge shock to the Conservative Party.

Table 10.2 Heywood and Middleton by-election results

Candidate	Party	Votes	% of vote	% change since 2010
McInnes	Labour	11,633	40.9	+0.8
Buckley	UKIP	11,016	38.7	+36.1
Gartside	Conservative	3,496	12.3	−14.9
Smith	Liberal Democrat	1,457	5.1	−17.6
Jackson	Green	870	3.0	+3.1

This was formerly a safe Labour seat. The result was very bad for the Conservatives and Liberal Democrats and excellent for UKIP, although they could not quite win the seat. Labour's performance drew differing interpretations. Some suggested it was a very poor result as they came so close to losing. However, Labour did win a larger share of the vote than they had done at the general election in 2010. The turnout, at 36%, was very low so it is possible that the close result was more because Labour supporters did not vote rather than the suggestion that there were voters who moved from Labour to UKIP. In other words, on a bigger turnout, Labour should increase their majority in 2015.

Table 10.3 Rochester and Strood by-election results

Candidate	Party	Votes	% of vote	% change since 2010
Reckless	UKIP	16,867	42.1	No candidate
Tolhurst	Conservative	13,947	34.8	−14.4
Khan	Labour	6,713	16.8	−11.7
Gregory	Green	1,692	4.2	+2.7
Juby	Liberal Democrat	349	0.9	−15.5
Others		497	1.2	N/A

This result was bad for the Conservatives but not the disaster predicted. However, unlike Clacton this was not considered promising country for UKIP, especially the middle-class Rochester part of the constituency. If anything like this result were to be replicated in the general election, the Conservatives would lose many seats to UKIP and certainly be unable to win power.

What are the implications of these dramatic results? They have a number of consequences:

- There may be more Conservative defections to UKIP. Many right-wing Conservatives will now fear that they will lose their seats at the general election. They may prefer to join UKIP and save their seats, rather than go down to defeat in 2015.
- It makes it extremely difficult to see how the Conservatives can win an overall majority in May 2015. This would be because they may lose seats to UKIP and, in places where there is a three-way contest (Conservative, Labour, UKIP), UKIP will split the right-wing vote and let Labour in, in seats which Conservatives would normally expect to win.
- The results are already having an impact on Conservative policy. David Cameron is talking tough on migration form EU countries. He is promising tax cuts for both those on low incomes and the better off, reducing the inheritance tax burden, raising the 40% rate of income tax to a threshold of £50,000 per annum and the 20% rate to £12,500. Many families would be hundreds of pounds per year better off.
- David Cameron has also renewed his threat to repeal the Human Rights Act, which is much criticised by UKIP, and replace it with a British Bill of Rights.

The main question now, though, is how much will these by-election results be replicated in the general election. Are they little more than protest votes or do they represent a genuine shift in political sentiment in Britain?

The executive: Baroness Warsi – a rare resignation

On 4 August 2014 Baroness Warsi, a junior Foreign Office minister, resigned from the government. At the time there was a major operation in the Palestinian territory of Gaza by Israeli forces who were seeking to prevent rocket attacks on their territory and to close down tunnels which were bringing terrorists from Gaza into Israel. There was widespread international condemnation of Israel's action, especially as so many Palestinian civilians were being killed, injured or made homeless. The British government refused to join in the condemnation of Israel and did little to provide humanitarian aid to Gaza.

Sayeeda Warsi was appointed to the Conservative Cabinet in 2010, having been made party chairperson. Though she lost her cabinet position later, she was still bound by collective responsibility as a junior minister. She was an especially important minister not least because she was from an unusual background in a political elite dominated by privately educated, white, middle-class males. Warsi ticked a number of 'inclusiveness' boxes, including:

- She is, of course, a woman.
- She is a Muslim.
- She is from the north of England.
- She is from a relatively poor background.

Her resignation demonstrates that the convention of **collective responsibility** still operates in British politics. This doctrine means that any minister who does not feel they can support government policy must resign or not speak out. Baroness Warsi was enraged by British policy over Gaza and said her conscience would not allow her to stay in government. The last major resignation of this kind occurred in 2003 when Labour Foreign Secretary, Robin Cook, resigned over Britain's involvement in the invasion of Iraq of that year. Shortly afterwards, International Development Secretary, Clare Short followed him, this time over the lack of follow-up aid in Iraq.

Warsi's loss is a blow to the government on several grounds:

- It highlights concerns over government policy in the Middle East.
- Warsi is a prominent Muslim. Her loss may result in many other Muslims abandoning support for the Conservative Party.
- The gender and ethnic balance of the government was disturbed by her loss. She was an important counterweight to the stereotypical nature of Cameron's team.
- She has a sizeable following in the Conservative Party. Her resignation weakens Cameron's control of the party.

Parliament: private member's legislation – rare successes

It is normally the case that we expect the government to develop legislation and Parliament to scrutinise and, on rare occasions, even veto it. There is a mechanism for individual members of either house of parliament to bring forward bills (Private Member's Bills), but it is rare for such proposals to succeed. 2014, however, has seen two such bills making good progress through Parliament.

A Private Member's Bill did succeed in 2012 when Lord Clement-Jones' **Live Music Bill**, supported by Liberal Democrat Don Foster in the Commons passed into law. This piece of legislation amended the existing regulations requiring music venues to seek a licence to operate. Critics argued that these regulations were killing off small venues which are so vital for the development of new talent. It succeeded because it had widespread support in both houses of parliament and the government saw no reason to oppose it.

The **Medical Innovation Bill**, sponsored by Lord (Maurice) Saatchi, proposes that doctors should be allowed to use untested and unapproved drugs in circumstances where a patient is certified as having less than six months to live and where all alternatives have been tried and have failed. The bill has widespread support and is now expected to pass into law in 2015, despite significant amendments having been added.

The **EU Referendum Bill**, sponsored by Conservative MP Robert Neill, will force Parliament to hold a referendum on the UK's membership of the European Union, a vote that was last held in 1975. This bill has the support of the prime minister and the Conservative Party as well as some Liberal Democrats. In October 2014 it passed its second reading unopposed. The government will be putting its resources behind it, though it may face problems on its way through the Commons and in the House of Lords. It is also true that, should there be a Labour Commons majority after 2015, the bill could be repealed and no referendum held. Parliamentary sovereignty means that each Parliament cannot bind its successors.

Both bills are helped by the fact that the 2014–15 session of Parliament is a light one, with little legislation going through, so there is plenty of time available. Private Member's Bills often fail not because of lack of support, but because there is insufficient parliamentary time to consider them. Government legislation always takes priority.

Political parties: Cameron goes for the middle-class vote

The new Conservative tax-cutting agenda

During the years of austerity, between 2008 and 2014, many of the middle classes have seen their standard of living reduced, largely because taxes on this economic group have drifted up (so-called 'fiscal drag'). The group has become known as the 'squeezed middle'. Faced by the gains being made by UKIP and the opinion polls that show the Conservatives still trailing Labour, David Cameron has decided to act, though it remains problematic whether he can carry through his policies.

In October 2014 he declared that he wished to reduce taxes in a number of ways. The main three that he suggested were:

1 The threshold for payment of inheritance tax should be raised to £1 million, taking the vast majority of people out of this tax.

2 Raising the level of income at which people *start* paying any tax at all should be raised to £12,500 per annum, from its current level of £10,500.

3 The income level at which taxpayers would start paying income tax at 40% should be raised from about £41,000 at present, to £50,000.

At the same time he declared his total opposition to the Labour/Liberal Democrat proposals for a 'mansion tax' which would be levied on owners of properties worth over £2 million.

The problem for Cameron is where he will get the money from to pay for such tax reductions, while, at the same time, the government is committed to eliminating the government budget deficit. Opponents, mostly on the left, claim that the tax cuts would be financed by cuts in benefits to poor working families. It may be that they remain ambitions rather than firm policies. Whatever occurs, it is clear that Cameron would like to bring the Conservative Party back to its traditional role as a 'tax-cutting party' and so recover its support from the middle classes, the place where they believe, elections are won and lost.

Parliament: IS in Iraq and Syria

Parliament takes control of British military policy in the Middle East
There is a developing story in the history of the uncodified and flexible UK constitution that can be traced back to the Iraq war in 2003. This concerns the prime minister's conventional position as commander-in-chief.

It has been the case for centuries that the prime minister enjoys the **prerogative power** to command Britain's armed forces. Parliament may give its opinion on his or her performance of this role, but has no constitutional power to control it – or so the theory went.

Under Tony Blair, British forces were deployed three times without prior parliamentary approval. These were an intervention in the civil war in Kosovo in 1999 on humanitarian grounds, a mission to help the democratic government of Sierra Leone which was threatened by a rebellion and which requested the troops, in May 2000, and the 2003 invasion, along with the USA, of Iraq, on the grounds that Saddam Hussein had weapons of mass destruction he was ready to use. In none of these cases was prior parliamentary approval sought by the government. The water was muddied in 2003 when a parliamentary vote was held *after* the deployment of troops in Iraq (it approved the action by a small majority), by which time it was too late.

In 2011 David Cameron ordered the RAF to intervene in the Libyan civil war in support of democratic rebels in Benghazi, which was in danger of falling. Like Blair in Iraq, he took the decision without asking parliament but did, several days later, obtain approval for the action. So change appeared to be on the way, but the prime minister's role had not yet been seriously challenged. All this changed, however, in 2013 when David Cameron *did* seek prior approval for a British intervention in the Syrian civil war. Parliament voted against the action and Cameron had to abandon the plan. Then in 2014 there were fresh calls for intervention by the air force in Iraq and Syria, where the forces of Islamic State (also known as ISIS or ISIL) were making huge territorial gains and terrorising large sections of the population. Learning from his experience the previous year Cameron took the issue to parliament again. This time Parliament took their role a stage further.

Aerial intervention against IS was approved but parliament insisted on two conditions. First, there was to be no intervention on Syrian territory and second, no ground troops were to be deployed. Thus Parliament was not only exercising its new powers, it was also succeeding in *directing* military policy.

Thus, as was reported in the 2014 Update, we are probably witnessing the development of a new constitutional convention. As things stand the convention could be described thus :

> The UK government shall seek the approval of the House of Commons in order to undertake any *significant* military action abroad.

The clear exceptions to this would be :

1 If a decision had to be taken at extremely short notice, leaving no time for parliamentary approval.

2 If an action had to be, by necessity, clandestine.

Constitutional experts remain divided on whether any such new convention has emerged. However, since Iraq in 2003, it is difficult to envisage a time when any major military action could be undertaken without parliamentary sanction. In other words, the flexible UK constitution seems to have succeeded in adapting itself to new circumstances without the need for legislation.